dip it!

Other books by Rick Rodgers

Barbecues 101

Best Barbecues Ever (with Irena Chalmers)

Best Ever Brownies (with Joan Steuer)

Best Ever Chocolate Desserts

Christmas 101

50 Best Stuffings and Dressings

Fondue: Great Food to Dip, Dunk, Savor, and Swirl

Fried & True

*Kaffeehaus: Exquisite Desserts from the Classic Cafés of
    Vienna, Budapest, and Prague*

*Mississippi Memories (with the Delta Queen Steamboat
    Company)*

Mr. Pasta's Healthy Pasta Cookbook

On Rice: 60 Toppings That Make the Meal

*The Perfect Parties Series: Picnics and Tailgate Parties;
    Bridal and Baby Showers; Romantic Dinners and
    Breakfasts; Birthday Celebrations*

Simply Shrimp

The Slow Cooker Ready & Waiting Cookbook

Thanksgiving 101

365 Ways to Cook Hamburger and Other Ground Meats

The Turkey Cookbook

Williams-Sonoma Collection: Chicken (with Chuck Williams)

Great Party Food to Spread,
Spoon, and Scoop

dip it!

RICK RODGERS

wm

WILLIAM MORROW
An Imprint of HarperCollins*Publishers*

HarperCollins books may be purchased for educational, business, or sales promotional use. For information please write: Special Markets Department, HarperCollins Publishers Inc., 10 East 53rd Street, New York, NY 10022.

FIRST EDITION

Designed by William Ruoto

Printed on acid-free paper

Library of Congress Cataloging-in-Publication Data has been applied for.

ISBN 0-06-000223-9

02   03   04   05   06   QW   10   9   8   7   6   5   4   3   2

For three people who know how to
party—Patrick, Mom, and Dad

Contents

Acknowledgments

The majority of names in my acknowledgments stays pretty much the same with every book. I am so lucky to have such a collection of people who are both dear friends and supportive colleagues.

Thanks to Diane Kniss and Steven Evasew, who have worked beside me in the kitchen for more than fifteen years. Kelly Volpe and David Bonom also helped out with recipe testing and recipe contributions. Diane Phillips is always there with a recipe suggestion and an email of encouragement. And Patrick Fisher never tired of my latest dips and chips.

It's a pleasure to be working with the gang at William Morrow, starting with my editor and cooking buddy, Harriet Bell, her assistant Karen Ferries, production editor Ann Cahn, copy editor Judith Sutton, production manager Karen Lumley, art director Roberto de Vicq de Cumptich, book designer William Ruoto, and publicist Carrie Weinberg. You really do seem like family. And as always, extra helpings of gratitude to Susan Ginsburg, my hard-working agent, and her gracious assistant, Annie Leuenberger.

The World
of Dips

Go to a party in any corner of the world, and you're
bound to find a heaping bowl of a savory semi-liquid
mixture served with something perfect for dipping,
dunking, slathering, or scooping. The dip can be fishy,
meaty, salty, garlicky, oniony, spicy . . . it doesn't really mat-
ter, because every kind is as good as the next. The things
that are dipped range from potato and tortilla chips to

fresh or toasted slices of bread to raw vegetables and beyond. Why are dips so popular? Simply because they are an easy, versatile, and tasty way to serve a crowd. And eating with your fingers is always relaxed and fun, the ultimate party icebreaker.

In this country, the dip is a twentieth-century invention. In *The American Century Cookbook*, Jean Anderson mentions evidence of a clam dip recipe from Mrs. Woodrow Wilson that dated back to around 1918. Anderson believes that it was James Beard's groundbreaking *Hors d'Oeuvre and Canapés*, published in 1940, that exposed a new generation of cooks to dips and set the stage for their rise to culinary fame.

Dips reached their apogee in the 1950s, when the larger homes of the new suburbia encouraged entertaining and cooks began to experiment with new foods. Old dip recipes always seem to start with a convenience food—an envelope or can of dried or condensed soup, a slab of pasteurized cheese product, a package of frozen vegetables—and they were stirred up in about the same time it took to tear open the bag of chips. Some of them were so delicious that they became American classics (you won't see me turning up my nose at my mom's onion soup dip, which is served at every Rodgers party, usually alongside my sister-in-law's seven-layer dip). But as the abilities of cooks improved and their tastes changed, many cooks began to consider the dip warhorses slightly quaint, or even outré.

At the same time, people became more familiar with the foreign cuisines that had served smooth and savory purees, sauces, and spreads as appetizers for centuries. Caponata, bagna cauda, and olivada from Italy; Provençal tapenade and aïoli; Thai peanut sauce; spicy Mexican salsas and guacamole; taramasalata, hummus, and baba ganoush from the eastern Mediterranean—all these entered America's culinary consciousness and recipe boxes. A party dip now meant something more than a carton of sour cream mixed with whatever was in the pantry, and dips acquired a new cachet.

This book explores all sides of the dip phenomenon. For cooks who are looking for nostalgic flavors without the preservatives and sodium found in processed foods, I offer updated, from-scratch versions of the classics. But for fun (and for cooks who simply want to take the easy way out—and need all of their dip recipes in one place), I also provide the "back of the box" recipes for the obvious suspects. I've come up with new dips for today's tastes, featuring ingredients that Mom didn't have at her disposal when she stirred up her first dip. I pay my respects to the classics of other countries, often adding twists that make them more special and appropriate for a party. And I've created more than a few dips that will become the ones you want to make for your next bash. You will find recipes for dips that are thicker than the typical sour cream-and-mayonnaise concoctions, and could officially be called spreads. Who cares? I say that if it can be scooped, slathered, or spread, it's a dip.

The Dynamics of Dips

Making a dip is as easy as can be—mix and serve. But there are a few basic tips that will perfect your dip-making skills.

• The number of servings depends on the appetites of the people who are doing the dipping. The guys dipping tortilla chips at a Super Bowl bash will probably eat more than a mixed crowd at a subdued cocktail party. In general, estimate ¼ cup dip per person.

• Stir the dip in a mixing bowl, not the serving bowl. Few serving bowls are large enough to allow for thorough blending of the ingredients. Transfer the mixed dip to a serving bowl, and always wipe away any drips.

• In most cases, tightly cover the bowl with plastic wrap and refrigerate to chill, or just long enough to blend the flavors. The plastic wrap keeps unwanted odors in the refrigerator from mingling with the dip (and vice versa).

• Most dips, but not all, benefit from a resting period before serving. Guacamole and some salsas are good examples of dips that are best served very soon after making; if they sit too long, the flavors get muddled. All of the recipes in this book come with make-ahead suggestions, and there are recommendations for reheating the hot dips.

• Because the flavors settle and mingle during the resting period, you should taste and reseason the dip before serving. The longer the rest, the more reseasoning may be necessary. Some dips may need a bit of salt and pepper, others a splash of lemon juice. Some dips made with processed foods may seem oversalted to today's tastes. These can often be rescued by stirring in sour cream (but not mayonnaise, which contains salt).

- Dips are meant to be indulgent party food, not everyday fare. Nonetheless, feel free to reduce the fat and calorie content of rich dips by using turkey bacon; low- or nonfat versions of mayonnaise, cream and Cheddar cheeses, or sour cream; and other similar products. I am not saying that the dips will taste the same, but if you are already cooking with these foods, the difference will be less noticeable. I prefer to mix low-fat products with regular ones so the change isn't so dramatic (reduced-fat mayonnaise with regular sour cream, for example.)

- Some dips thicken when chilled. If a dip becomes too thick to scoop, thin it with an appropriate liquid, preferably one used in the recipe. Sour cream–based dips thin nicely with a splash of milk. Others work better with broth, olive oil, or water.

- Dips that contain mayonnaise, raw eggs, meats, or fish should not sit at room temperature for longer than 2 hours. When necessary, replace the bowl of dip with a fresh, cold batch. Here are two ways for keeping a dip cold.

  Scoop out a 1½-pound round loaf of bread to make a bowl. Freeze for 3 hours, then fill. The bread bowl will keep the dip cold for about 3 hours.

  Place the serving bowl in an attractive baking dish and surround it with cracked ice or ice cubes. Place the baking dish on a thick towel or platter to catch any condensation.

- If you are looking for a hot dip, note the 🍲 icon in the dip's title.

- There are many options for keeping hot dips warm. I prefer to use a shallow ceramic fondue pot (the kind used for cheese fondue, also called a *caquelon*) for most dips. It can go into the oven and absorbs the heat so well that it will keep the dip hot for an hour or so during serving without auxiliary heat. For longer periods, place the fondue pot on its stand and keep warm over a flame. Some dips may scorch on the bottom if overheated, so keep the flame very low or even substitute a votive candle for the heating element. A 1-quart mini–slow cooker (bake the dip right in the crockery insert) or a hot plate are good alternatives, but their use is restricted by the location of your electric outlets.

- Don't forget the garnish! Many a delicious dip could use a little help in the looks department. A sprinkle of paprika, a drizzle of olive oil or heavy cream, chopped fresh herbs (or just a sprig), a dollop of sour cream or yogurt—all of these have been called into duty to beautify a homely dip.

- When serving dips, think outside of the box (or should I say "outside of the bowl"?). If you are using a bowl, choose one that is brightly colored to set off the dip. Hollowed-out loaves of bread, heads of cabbage (preferably with large floppy outside leaves still attached), and dramatic-looking winter squash all make terrific dip holders.

Glossary of Ingredients and Techniques

Here are some ingredients and cooking techniques for dips that might be unfamiliar or need a little explanation.

AVOCADOS Always use Hass avocados, the variety with dark, pebbly skin. Large Florida avocados with shiny green skin are watery and flavorless. A ripe avocado will yield to gentle squeezing, but it shouldn't be squishy. Unripe, hard avocados have an olive green skin. They can be ripened at room temperature in a closed paper bag for a few days.

To pit an avocado, cut it lengthwise in half. Twist the two halves while pulling them apart to reveal the pit, which will remain attached to one half. Using a heavy knife, rap the pit with the blade, which should stick into the pit. Twist the knife to release and remove the pit. (You can also dig the pit out with a spoon, but that is a slippery way to go.)

To peel the avocado, scoop the flesh out of each half with a large serving spoon. The flesh is now ready for chopping or mashing.

CHILES, DRIED AND FRESH   Gone are the days when the only way a cook could get heat into food was with a sprinkle of cayenne pepper or the occasional can of green chiles. Chiles range in heat from relatively mild to very, very hot. Dried ancho chiles have a fruity sweetness to them, whereas chipotle chiles will set your mouth on fire. All manner of dried and fresh chiles are available at Latino grocers and many supermarkets. A great mail-order source for dried chiles is Kitchen Food Shop, 218 Eighth Avenue, New York, NY 10011; (212) 243-4433; www.kitchenmarket.com.

Chiles must be treated with respect, as their oils can easily burn more areas of your body than your mouth. If your skin is especially tender, wear rubber gloves. In any case, don't touch tender parts of your body, especially your eyes, until you have thoroughly washed your hands.

The ribs and seeds are the hottest parts of the chile, so they are usually removed before chopping. That doesn't mean they are inedible. In fact, reserve them until after you have tasted the dip. If you think it needs a bit more heat, sprinkle in the seeds. In extreme cases, you can mince the ribs and add them to the dip. All dried chiles are usually toasted in a skillet before using to bring out their flavor.

The chiles used in this book are:

Ancho   The dried version of the poblano chile (some brands label them dried poblanos).

Chipotle   A smoked jalapeño. The dehydration of these chiles during the smoking process intensifies their heat. While they can be found dried, they are most often canned in a chile sauce (adobo).

Jalapeño   The most familiar chile, with a relatively hot flavor profile. Serrano chiles, which are smaller, can be substituted.

Poblano   A dark green, oval chile with a pointed tip. Usually on the mild side, these are great for roasting. Similar mild chiles include the New Mexico and Anaheim varieties. You should be able to find at least one of these at a Latino market.

To roast fresh poblanos and other mild chiles, position the broiler rack 6 inches from the source of heat and preheat the broiler. Lay the whole chiles on the broiler rack. (While I like to cut open bell peppers before roasting so they will lie flat, the irregular shape of chile peppers makes that impossible.) Broil, turning occasionally, until the skin is charred on all sides, about 10 minutes. Do not char the skin too much, or you will burn the flesh. Transfer the chiles to a bowl and cover tightly with plastic wrap. Let stand and steam until cool enough to handle, about 20 minutes. Pull off the blackened skin, scraping away stubborn areas with a paring knife. Do not rinse the chiles under cold water, as this would rinse away much of the flavor. Discard the seeds and ribs, and chop the chiles as directed in the recipe.

CUMIN SEEDS This aromatic spice is popular in Mexican and Middle Eastern cooking. Ground cumin is available at every supermarket, but toasting whole cumin seeds and grinding them yourself results in better flavor (toasting brings out the spice's oils, so they have more impact).

To toast cumin seeds, place them in a small skillet over medium heat. Heat, stirring occasionally, until very fragrant and toasted (you may see a wisp of smoke), 2 to 3 minutes. Immediately turn out of the skillet onto a plate and cool completely. Grind with a mortar and pestle or in an electric coffee grinder.

GARLIC As the cloves from this little bulb flavor so many dips, it is worth a few words. Use fresh garlic, never the chopped garlic packed in oil, which tastes processed. I use a garlic press for many recipes because I don't want little nibs of garlic in the dip. (Because crushing in a press exposes more of the garlic's oils to the air, it is true that a press increases the garlic flavor, something that some cooks consider undesirable. But I figure that if I am using garlic, I want to taste garlic.)

Roasted garlic is all about mellowness, not strength. *To roast garlic,* cut off the top of a large, plump head of garlic to make a lid. Drizzle the cut bottom portion with a few drops of olive oil and season with a pinch each of salt and pepper. Replace the lid, reforming the head of garlic, and wrap in aluminum foil. Roast in a preheated 400°F oven until the garlic feels soft when squeezed, about 40 minutes. Cool completely before using, then squeeze out the pulp.

MAYONNAISE   Since mayonnaise is an essential ingredient for many dips, don't skimp and get an inexpensive brand with potentially disappointing flavor. Buy a reputable brand, such as Best Foods, Hellmann's, or Kraft, and you'll be glad you did.

ONIONS, GRATED   Grated onions add flavor without the not-always-pleasant texture of chopped onions. Simply grate the onion on the large holes of a box grater. You'll be surprised to find that a whole small onion grates down to just a couple of tablespoons.

PORCINI MUSHROOM POWDER   When you want to add the distinctive flavor of porcini mushrooms to a dish but don't have the time for the traditional soaking, sprinkle in some porcini mushroom powder. Available at specialty markets, it's nothing more than ground dried porcini mushrooms. You can make your own by grinding porcini mushrooms in an electric coffee grinder or mini–food processor until pulverized. If you buy dried porcini in large bags (as I always do, because it saves money, and they keep for months), this is a great way to use up the tiny broken bits in the bottom of the bag.

RED PEPPERS, ROASTED   Why bother to roast a pepper? The heat parcooks the pepper's flesh, mellows the flavor, and chars the bitter skin so it can easily be peeled away. There are a lot of different ways to roast a pepper, usually involving the chore of turning and charring the pepper over an open flame. I have always found this an inefficient, tedious method, and much prefer to cut up the pepper so it lies flat and can be broiled without turning.

To roast bell peppers, cut off the top ½ inch of the pepper (including the stem), then cut off the bottom ½ inch. Place the top and bottom sections on a broiling pan. Make an incision down the side of the pepper, and open it out to make a strip, skin side down. Cut away and discard the ribs and seeds.

Position the broiler rack 6 inches from the heat source and preheat the broiler. Place the pepper skin side up on the broiler rack. Broil until most of the skin is charred black, being careful not to char the skin so much that you burn the flesh, about 10 minutes, depending on the heat of the broiler. (The peppers can also be grilled outdoors over high heat in a covered charcoal or gas grill.) Remove the pan from the oven and cover with foil. Let stand until the peppers are cool enough to handle, about 20 minutes.

Peel off and discard the charred skin. Use a small sharp knife to help remove stubborn patches of skin or scrape off overly blackened areas. Do not rinse the peppers under cold water, which would wash away flavor. Don't worry about getting rid of every bit of blackened skin—a bit of charred skin will add character.

TAHINI Sesame seeds ground into a paste, tahini can be found at Mediterranean grocers, specialty food shops, and most supermarkets. It adds a smooth, nutty flavor to many dips. In recipes that use a small amount (up to ¼ cup), you can substitute smooth peanut butter.

When you open a jar or can of tahini, you'll find an oily layer that has separated from the paste during storage, which is not easy to stir back into the tahini. Here's a trick I learned from my friend David Bonom: Scrape all of the tahini in a food processor or blender and whirl it to re-emulsify. Now scrape the blended tahini back into the jar for storage in the refrigerator. It will take another month or so before the oil separates again.

TOMATOES, SALTED   Some recipes ask you to salt tomatoes before using them. This is a great trick, as it drains off excess liquid that would otherwise dilute the dip. The salting also seasons the tomato cubes.

New and Old Favorites

When I was a caterer, a terrific dip was a surefire way to get compliments on the food. Even at parties that offered gorgeous, intricately crafted hors d'oeuvres, it was the dip that had guests peeking into the kitchen to ask for the recipe. I know why. Not only do people like the communal aspect of serving dips but they are sure to be able to reproduce the recipes at home.

Most cooks feel that ease of preparation is a requirement for a good dip. Many favorite dips start with opening an envelope of dried soup mix, and I've made many a dip that way myself. But my goal is to provide you with the *best* version of a recipe, even if it requires a couple of extra steps. When I serve from-scratch versions of onion, spinach, clam, or artichoke dip, my guests can definitely tell the difference. And it shows that I care enough about them to make a special effort. None of these dips will exhaust you. And all of them will be worth the little bit of extra effort. (Where appropriate, though, I have also given the mix-and-serve recipes.)

Real Onion Dip

makes about 2 cups

MAKE-AHEAD: The dip can be prepared up to 2 days ahead.

Anyone who's ever given a party surely knows how to make California Dip, probably America's favorite dip, with an envelope of onion soup mix and a carton of sour cream. (According to the Lipton Company, who prints the recipe on every box of their dried onion soup, it is called California Dip because an anonymous homemaker from that state invented it.) My version, freshly made with caramelized onions replacing the dehydrated ones, challenges the classic with a fuller, less salty flavor. Serve this with homemade potato chips, and get ready for the compliments.

what to dip

Potato chips, store-bought or homemade (page 171 or 174) • Broccoli and cauliflower florets, prepared for dipping (see page 85) • Carrot sticks • Celery sticks • Cucumber slices • Tiny new potatoes, cooked (see page 87) • Zucchini rounds

2 tablespoons vegetable oil
2 medium onions, chopped (3 cups)
¾ cup mayonnaise
¾ cup sour cream
Salt and freshly ground black pepper
Finely chopped fresh chives for garnish

1. Heat the oil in a large skillet over medium-low heat. Add the onions, cover, and cook, stirring occasionally, until

golden, about 20 minutes. Uncover and continue cooking, stirring often, until deep golden brown, 15 to 20 minutes. Cool completely.

2. Mix the mayonnaise and sour cream in a medium bowl. Stir in the onions. Season with salt and pepper. Cover and refrigerate until chilled, at least 2 hours, or up to 2 days. (If necessary, thin with milk before serving.)

3. Transfer to a serving bowl and sprinkle with chives. Serve chilled or at room temperature.

BLUE CHEESE AND ONION DIP   Mash 4 ounces Roquefort or Danish blue cheese, crumbled, into the mayonnaise–sour cream mixture.

ORIGINAL CALIFORNIA DIP   Mix 1 envelope Lipton Onion Recipe Soup Mix with one 16-ounce container sour cream. Cover and chill for at least 30 minutes.

Hot Artichoke and Dill Dip

makes 2¾ cups

MAKE-AHEAD: The dip can be prepared up to 1 day ahead, then baked just before serving.

I grew up not far from Castroville, known as the Artichoke Capital of the World. I well remember weekend morning rides along the California coast when road stands sold artichokes for a nickel each, and our lunches with mountains of boiled artichokes and mayonnaise. When artichoke dip became popular in the sixties (promoted by Best Foods as a way to cook with their Hellmann's/Best Foods mayonnaise), I fell in love immediately, as it featured one of my favorite food combinations. Here is my offering for the perfect artichoke dip.

what to dip

Potato chips, store-bought or homemade (page 171 or 174) • Baguette slices • Crostini (page 180) • Pita bread wedges • Pita Toasts (page 179) • Breadsticks, store-bought or homemade (page 184) • Cooked artichoke leaves, reserved from the recipe • Celery sticks • Zucchini rounds

4 medium globe artichokes
(about 10 ounces each),
preferably with stems
attached
1½ cups (6 ounces) shredded havarti or Monterey Jack
¾ cup freshly grated Parmesan
¾ cup mayonnaise

1½ tablespoons chopped fresh dill
1 garlic clove, crushed through a press
⅓ cup fresh bread crumbs (whirl crusty bread in the
  blender or food processor)
2 teaspoons olive oil

1. Bring a large pot of lightly salted water to a boil over high heat. Add the artichokes and place a heatproof bowl or plate on top to keep them submerged. Cook until the artichokes are very tender and the leaves are easy to pull off, 45 minutes to 1 hour. Drain and rinse under cold water until cool enough to handle.

2. Working with one artichoke at a time, pull off the leaves until you reach the thin core of very tender leaves. Place the leaves in a plastic bag and refrigerate to serve with the dip, if desired. Pull off the core to reveal the heart. Using a dessert spoon, scoop out and discard the fuzzy choke. Using a small sharp knife, trim off any tough skin from the hearts and the stems, if attached (the inner stem has the same flavor as the heart). Chop the heart and stems into ½-inch cubes.

3. Mix the chopped artichoke, havarti, Parmesan, mayonnaise, dill, and garlic in a medium bowl. Transfer to a 3- to 4-cup baking dish. (The dip can be covered and refrigerated for up to 1 day.)

4. Position a rack in the center of the oven and preheat the oven to 350°F.

5. Sprinkle the bread crumbs on the dip and drizzle with the oil. Bake until the dip is bubbling, 20 to 30 minutes (longer if it's been refrigerated). Serve hot.

ORIGINAL ARTICHOKE DIP   Mix ½ cup Hellmann's or Best Foods mayonnaise, ½ cup sour cream, one 14-ounce can artichoke hearts, drained and chopped, ⅓ cup freshly grated Parmesan, and ⅛ teaspoon hot red pepper sauce. Bake as directed.

Spinach-Leek Dip

makes 3 cups

MAKE-AHEAD: The dip can be prepared up to 2 days ahead.

The classic spinach dip, like so many other favorite dips and dunks, starts with an envelope of dried soup mix (you'll find the classic recipe on every package of Knorr Vegetable Soup, Dip, and Recipe Mix). I have served the mix-and-serve version often, simply because everyone loves it so much, and I include the recipe here. But when I serve my friend Diane Kniss's recipe (see the variation), they line up at the dip bowl! I also enjoy making this tarragon-scented rendition with fresh vegetables, and it too has the party guests licking the bowl.

what to dip

Potato chips, store-bought or homemade (page 171 or 174) • Broccoli and cauliflower florets, prepared for dipping (see page 85) • Carrot sticks • Celery sticks • Cucumber slices • Tiny new potatoes, cooked (see page 87) • Zucchini rounds

4 teaspoons olive oil
Two 6-ounce bags baby spinach
1 cup thinly sliced leeks (white part only)
½ cup finely chopped red bell pepper
¼ cup chopped shallots
2 garlic cloves, minced
Salt and freshly ground black pepper to taste
1 cup sour cream

1 cup mayonnaise
1 tablespoon chopped fresh dill or 1 teaspoon dried dill
⅛ teaspoon ground hot red (cayenne) pepper

1. Heat 2 teaspoons of the oil in a large nonstick skillet over medium heat. In batches, stir in the spinach, wilting each batch before adding more. Sprinkle the spinach with 1 tablespoon water, cover, and cook until the spinach is tender, about 5 minutes. Drain, rinse, and cool. A handful at a time, squeeze the excess liquid from the spinach. Chop coarsely.

2. Heat the remaining 2 teaspoons oil in the skillet over medium heat. Add the leeks and red pepper and cook, stirring often, until softened, about 3 minutes. Stir in the shallots and garlic and cook, stirring often, until softened, about 2 minutes. Cool completely.

3. Combine the spinach, cooled vegetables, sour cream, mayonnaise, dill, and cayenne in a food processor and process until blended. Season with salt and pepper. Transfer to a bowl and cover tightly. Refrigerate until chilled, at least 2 hours, or up to 2 days.

4. Serve chilled.

CLASSIC SPINACH DIP Mix one-ounce container sour cream, 1 cup mayonnaise, one 10-ounce package frozen chopped spinach, thawed and squeezed to remove excess moisture, 3 chopped scallions (white and green parts), and one 1.4-ounce envelope Knorr Vegetable Soup, Dip, and Recipe Mix. Cover and chill. Makes 3 cups.

DIANE'S DELUXE SPINACH DIP Mix one 16-ounce container sour cream, 2 cups mayonnaise, one 10-ounce package frozen chopped spinach, thawed and squeezed to remove excess moisture, ½ cup chopped scallions, ½ cup chopped fresh parsley, ½ cup chopped fresh dill, one 1.4-ounce package Knorr Vegetable Soup, Dip, and Recipe Mix, and 1 tablespoon cheese-based salad seasoning (such as Salad Supreme). Cover and chill. Makes 5½ cups.

Chile con Queso

makes about 4 cups

MAKE-AHEAD: The vegetables for the dip can be prepared up to 8 hours ahead; the dip is best served as soon as it is made.

Unfortunately, many chile con queso recipes don't live up to the true meaning of the name—it should be chiles with cheese, (not cheese with chiles) and a good amount of fresh, mild chiles is in order. While some north of the border cooks swear by processed cheese (which does melt smoothly and resists separating), a combination of Monterey Jack and Cheddar gives great results. The dip tends to separate if overheated, so keep it warm at the very lowest heat level, or make and serve it in batches to keep it looking its best.

what to dip

Tortilla chips, store-bought or homemade (page 176) • Broccoli florets, prepared for dipping (see page 85) • Cherry tomatoes • Mushroom caps • Zucchini wedges

1 tablespoon olive oil
1 medium onion, finely chopped
1 jalapeño, seeded and minced
2 garlic cloves, minced
One 15-ounce can diced tomatoes in juice, drained
3 mild chiles, such as Anaheim, New Mexico, or
    poblanos, roasted (see page 9), peeled, seeded, and
    chopped

½ cup heavy cream
1½ cups (6 ounces) shredded Monterey Jack
1½ cups (6 ounces) shredded sharp Cheddar
1 tablespoon cornstarch

1. Heat the oil in a large skillet over medium heat. Add the onion and jalapeño and cook, stirring often, until the onion is translucent, about 5 minutes. Add the garlic and stir until fragrant, about 1 minute. Stir in the tomatoes and cook until they give off their juices, about 3 minutes. (The dip can be prepared to this point up to 8 hours ahead, cooled, covered, and refrigerated. Reheat in the skillet over medium heat.) Stir in the cream and bring to a simmer. Reduce the heat to low. Toss the Monterey Jack and Cheddar with the cornstarch in a medium bowl. Gradually whisk the cheese into the skillet and bring to a simmer.

2. Transfer to a heatproof serving dish and serve hot.

CHILE CON QUESO CON CHORIZO   Cut 4 smoked chorizo links (about 3 ounces) into ¼-inch dice. Cook the chorizo in the oil over medium heat, stirring often, until browned, about 5 minutes. Add the onion and jalapeño to the chorizo and its drippings and continue as directed.

Rosemary Aïoli

makes about 1¾ cups

MAKE-AHEAD: The dip can be prepared up to 3 days ahead.

Aïoli simply is garlic mayonnaise, but to the citizens of Provence, it represents the very soul of their cuisine. Many Provencal communities serve a huge feast (usually as fundraisers for a church or some other charity) called *la grande aïoli*, where salt cod, snails, braised meats and chicken, and a mountain of vegetables are served family-style for dipping into the aromatic *raison d'être*. Purists will warn that aïoli must always be made by hand in a mortar and pestle, but once I peeked into the staging area of a grande aïoli, only to see the cooks making theirs with a food processor, so I have no guilt in recommending you do the same. A bit of boiling water gives the aïoli a creamier texture.

what to dip

Baguette slices • Crostini (page 180) • Breadsticks, store-bought or homemade (page 184) • Baby artichoke hearts, cooked (page 84) • Carrot sticks • Celery sticks • Cherry tomatoes • Fennel bulb, cut into sticks • Tiny new potatoes, cooked (see page 87) • Red bell pepper strips • Zucchini rounds

1 cup vegetable oil
½ cup olive oil (not extra-virgin)
1 large egg, at room temperature (see Note)
1 tablespoon fresh lemon juice
4 garlic cloves, crushed through a press

1 tablespoon boiling water
1½ teaspoons chopped fresh rosemary
Salt and freshly ground black pepper to taste

1. Combine the vegetable and olive oils in a glass measuring cup. Place the egg, lemon juice, and garlic in a food processor and pulse to combine. With the processor running, gradually add the oil, drop by drop, to make a thick mayonnaise (it should take about 1 minute to add the oil). Add the water and rosemary and process to combine. Season with salt and pepper. Transfer to a bowl, cover, and refrigerate to blend the flavors, at least 2 hours, or up to 2 days.

2. Transfer to a serving bowl and serve chilled.

NOTE: This recipe uses raw egg. Very rarely, raw eggs have been known to contain the salmonella bacterium. To avoid possible contamination, use only fresh, uncracked eggs. Do not serve foods made with raw eggs to people with impaired immunity, the elderly, pregnant women, or the very young.

ROUILLE Traditionally served as a condiment for bouillabaisse, rouille (meaning "rust" in French, for its color) also makes a fine dip. Whisk 1 tablespoon tomato paste and ¼ teaspoon hot red (cayenne) pepper into the aïoli.

OLIVE AÏOLI Stir 2 tablespoons Tapenade (page 46) or store-bought olive paste into the aïoli.

Baba Ganoush

makes 4 cups

MAKE-AHEAD: The dip can be prepared up to 2 days ahead.

Eggplant dips are served with many variations through-
out the Mideast, but this one is the gold standard.
Grilling imparts a mild smokiness
to the eggplant flesh. However, you
can also roast the eggplants in a
preheated 400°F oven until they
collapse, about 40 minutes.

what to dip

Pita bread wedges •
Pita Toasts (page 179) •
Carrot sticks • Celery
sticks • Cherry
tomatoes • Cucumber
slices • Zucchini slices

2 large eggplants (about
   2 pounds each)
¼ cup tahini
3 tablespoons fresh lemon juice
2 tablespoons chopped fresh parsley, plus more for
   garnish
1 teaspoon ground cumin
3 garlic cloves, crushed through a press

1. Build a charcoal fire in an outdoor grill and let burn
until the coals are covered with white ash. Or preheat a gas
grill on High, then reduce the heat to Medium.

2. Grill the eggplants, turning occasionally, until they collapse and their skins are blackened and blistered, about 20
minutes. Let cool.

3. Cut the eggplants lengthwise in half and scoop the soft flesh from the skins into a bowl; discard the skins. Transfer the eggplant to a food processor, add the tahini, lemon juice, parsley, cumin, and garlic, and process to a puree. Transfer to a serving bowl, cover, and refrigerate to blend the flavors, at least 2 hours, or up to 2 days.

4. Sprinkle the top with the parsley and serve chilled or at room temperature.

Truffled Bagna Cauda

makes about 1 cup

MAKE-AHEAD: Bagna cauda is best served as soon as it is prepared.

Bagna cauda, a blend of oil, butter, anchovies, and garlic served warm, is not a mild-mannered dip. It is a specialty of Piedmont, a region of Italy also known for its truffles, and thinly sliced truffles are sometimes added to the pot. As truffles are not easily obtained in America, I use white truffle oil, which can be found at specialty grocers. Chill the vegetables well, so they will cool the hot dip before it finds its way into your guests' mouths.

> ## what to dip
>
> Baby artichoke hearts, cooked • Broccoli and cauliflower florets, prepared for dipping (see page 85) • Celery sticks • Cherry tomatoes • Fennel bulb, cut into sticks • Mushroom caps • Tiny new potatoes, cooked (see page 87) • Red bell pepper strips

5 tablespoons extra-virgin olive oil

6 anchovy fillets, finely chopped

3 garlic cloves, finely chopped

8 tablespoons (1 stick) unsalted butter

1 teaspoon white truffle oil, or more to taste

Freshly ground black pepper to taste

1. Combine 2 tablespoons of the oil, the anchovies, and garlic in a medium saucepan. Cook over medium heat, stir-

ring often, until the garlic is softened and the anchovies are dissolved, about 3 minutes.

2. Add the remaining 3 tablespoons oil and the butter and heat, stirring often, until the butter is melted. Stir in the truffle oil and season with salt and pepper. Transfer to a small fondue pot and keep warm over a low flame. Serve hot, with chilled crudités.

Blue Cheese Dip

makes about 2¼ cups

MAKE-AHEAD: The dip can be made up to 2 days ahead.

Every blue cheese has a flavor and texture that makes it unique, from the creamy richness of Gorgonzola to the crumbly sharpness of Danish blue. Use your favorite blue cheese to make this creamy dip, which is so thick you can stand a carrot stick up in it.

¾ cup mayonnaise
¾ cup sour cream
6 ounces blue cheese, crumbled
1 scallion, white and green
    parts, finely chopped
2 tablespoons fresh lemon juice
½ teaspoon celery seeds
1 garlic clove, crushed through
    a press
¼ teaspoon freshly ground black pepper

what to dip

Potato chips, store-bought or homemade (page 171 or 174) • Broccoli and cauliflower florets, prepared for dipping (see page 85) • Carrot sticks • Celery sticks • Cherry tomatoes • Cucumber slices • Zucchini slices

1. With a rubber spatula, mash the mayonnaise, sour cream, and cheese together in a medium bowl. Stir in the scallion, lemon juice, celery seeds, garlic, and pepper. Cover and refrigerate to blend the flavors, at least 2 hours or up to 2 days.

2. Transfer to a serving bowl and serve chilled.

Caponata

makes about 7 cups

MAKE-AHEAD: The caponata can be prepared up to 5 days ahead.

This is one of my most requested recipes, one that I perfected while making tons of it during my years as a caterer. It definitely improves after a day or two, a convenience that is not lost on busy hosts and hostesses. While most of us think of caponata as "Italian eggplant dip," it actually is named for the capers in the recipe.

> ### what to dip
>
> Crostini (page 180) •
> Bruschetta (page 182) •
> Flatbread crisps •
> Focaccia, cut into bite-sized pieces

1 large eggplant, about 2
    pounds, cut into ¾-inch cubes
Salt
½ cup extra-virgin olive oil
1 large onion, chopped
3 medium carrots, cut into ½-inch dice
3 medium celery ribs, cut into ½-inch dice
2 medium zucchini, cut into ½-inch dice
1 large red bell pepper, cored, seeded, and cut into ½-inch dice
3 garlic cloves, minced
One 28-ounce can tomatoes in juice, chopped, juice reserved

2 tablespoons red wine vinegar

2 tablespoons sugar

1 teaspoon dried basil

½ teaspoon dried oregano

½ teaspoon dried thyme

¼ teaspoon crushed hot red pepper

½ cup pitted and chopped Mediterranean black or
green olives (or use both)

3 tablespoons nonpareil capers, drained and rinsed

⅓ cup pine nuts, toasted

1.   Toss the eggplant with 1 tablespoon salt in a colander. Let stand in the sink for 1 to 2 hours to drain off excess moisture. Rinse the eggplant under cold running water, then pat dry with paper towels.

2.   Meanwhile, heat 3 tablespoons of the oil in a large heavy saucepan over medium heat. Add the onion, carrots, celery, zucchini, and bell pepper and cook, stirring often, until softened, about 10 minutes. Stir in the garlic and cook until fragrant, about 2 minutes. Add the tomatoes with their juice, the vinegar, sugar, basil, oregano, thyme, and red pepper. Bring to a simmer.

3.   Meanwhile, heat the remaining 5 tablespoons oil in a very large nonstick skillet over medium-high heat until very hot but not smoking. Add the eggplant and cook, turning occasionally, until browned, about 6 minutes. (If necessary, do this in batches, using more oil as needed.)

4. Stir the eggplant into the tomato sauce and bring to a simmer over medium heat. Reduce the heat to medium-low and simmer uncovered, stirring occasionally, until the vegetables are very tender, about 30 minutes. During the last 5 minutes, stir in the olives and capers. Remove from the heat and let cool completely. Transfer to a serving bowl, cover, and refrigerate until chilled, at least 4 hours, or up to 5 days.

5. Season with salt to taste. Sprinkle with the pine nuts. Serve chilled or at room temperature, with a small knife for spreading.

Buttermilk-Garlic Dip

makes about 1 cup

MAKE-AHEAD: The dip can be made up to 3 days ahead.

Garlicky buttermilk ranch dressing has somewhat cloudy origins. According to Jean Anderson's *American Century Cookbook* (Clarkson Potter, 1997), it could have been invented as a dip for the fried zucchini sticks at Bobby McGee's Restaurants in the 1980s, or it could be the brainchild of the Henson family, owners of the Hidden Valley Ranch near Santa Barbara, California. You find envelopes of ranch-style salad dressing–dip mix at the supermarket, but the recipe has to have been made from scratch at some point! Dried buttermilk powder, now a staple at most markets, gives the dip its authoritative tang without diluting the flavor of the ingredients.

what to dip

Potato chips, store-bought or homemade (page 171 or 174) • Frozen artichoke hearts, thawed • Broccoli and cauliflower florets, prepared for dipping (see page 85) • Carrot sticks • Celery sticks • Cherry tomatoes • Cucumber slices • Zucchini slices

½ cup mayonnaise
½ cup sour cream
3 tablespoons dried buttermilk powder
2 tablespoons chopped fresh parsley
1 tablespoon grated onion

1 garlic clove, crushed through a press
½ teaspoon dried thyme
½ teaspoon celery seeds
¼ teaspoon freshly ground black pepper

1. Whisk the mayonnaise, sour cream, and buttermilk powder in a medium bowl until the powder dissolves. Stir in the parsley, onion, garlic, thyme, celery seeds, and pepper. Cover and refrigerate to blend the flavors, at least 2 hours, or up to 3 days.

2. Transfer to a serving bowl and serve chilled.

Hummus bi Tahini

makes 1½ cups

MAKE-AHEAD: The hummus can be made up to 3 days ahead.

Hummus used to be considered an exotic dish only available in college towns with Middle Eastern restaurants or delis (I ate mountains of it when I lived near Berkeley). Now you can buy hummus at the supermarket. This authentic version includes tahini, which adds a delicious nuttiness to the dip. Play around with the seasonings, adding lemon juice, garlic, cumin, and/or cayenne to suit your taste.

what to dip

Pita bread wedges • Pita Toasts (page 179) • Broccoli florets, prepared for dipping (see page 85) • Carrot sticks • Celery sticks • Cherry tomatoes • Cucumber slices • Radishes

One 15½-ounce can garbanzo beans (chickpeas), drained, liquid reserved
¼ cup fresh lemon juice
3 tablespoons tahini
1 garlic clove, crushed through a press, or more to taste
½ teaspoon ground cumin
¼ cup extra-virgin olive oil, plus more for garnish
Salt and ground hot red (cayenne) pepper to taste
Paprika for garnish

1.   Combine the beans, lemon juice, tahini, garlic, and cumin in a food processor and puree. With the processor running, add ¼ cup of the oil, then enough of the bean liquid (about ¼ cup) to make the hummus smooth and fluffy. Season with salt and red pepper. Transfer to a bowl, cover, and refrigerate to blend the flavors, at least 1 hour, or up to 3 days.

2.   Mound the hummus in a serving bowl. Using the back of a tablespoon, make an indentation in the center, and fill it with a spoonful of oil. Sprinkle paprika over the top. Serve at room temperature.

HERBED HUMMUS   Omit the cumin. Add 2 teaspoons chopped fresh thyme or rosemary or 2 tablespoons chopped fresh basil or cilantro to the hummus.

RED PEPPER HUMMUS   Puree 1 roasted, peeled, and seeded red bell pepper (see page 12) with the beans.

Wild Mushroom Caviar

makes about 2 cups

MAKE-AHEAD: The mushroom caviar can be prepared up to 2 days ahead.

Ubiquitous on the appetizer menus of central Europe, mushroom caviar can be a bit predictable. In this version, a dash of dried porcini mushroom powder gives it a jolt of flavor. Cremini and shiitake mushrooms will lend an earthier taste than plain button mushrooms alone. Coarsely chop the mushrooms by hand before finely chopping in a food processor—you'll get a more uniform result.

what to spread

Baguette slices •
Crostini (page 180) •
Pita bread wedges •
Pita Toasts (page 179) •
Cucumber slices

1 pound assorted mushrooms, such as cremini and
   stemmed shiitakes, coarsely chopped
2 tablespoons unsalted butter
2 tablespoons fresh lemon juice
2 teaspoons dried porcini mushroom powder
   (see page 11)
1 tablespoon chopped fresh dill, plus more for garnish
⅓ cup finely chopped shallots
⅔ cup sour cream, plus more for garnish
⅛ teaspoon ground hot red (cayenne) pepper
Salt and freshly ground black pepper to taste

1. Pulse the mushrooms in a food processor until finely chopped but not pureed.

2. Melt the butter in a large skillet over medium-high heat. Add the mushrooms, then stir in the lemon juice, being sure to mix well (the lemon juice prevents the mushrooms from turning dark), the mushroom powder, and dill. Cook uncovered, stirring often, until the mushrooms give off their juices and they evaporate, about 6 minutes. Stir in the shallots and cook until softened, about 2 minutes. Remove from the heat and let cool completely.

3. Transfer the mushrooms to a bowl. Stir in the sour cream and red pepper. Season with salt and black pepper. Cover and refrigerate until chilled, at least 2 hours, or up to 2 days.

4. Transfer to a serving bowl and top with a dollop of sour cream. Sprinkle with chopped dill. Serve chilled or at room temperature, with a small knife for spreading.

Green Olivada

MAKE-AHEAD: The olivada can be prepared up to 1 week ahead.

At first glance, olivada and tapenade seem almost similar: both are highly seasoned olive pastes. However, tapenade must always include capers (in Provençal dialect, caper is *tapenado*). Great olivada requires great green olives, so look for the meatiest, most flavorful green ones available.

> **what to dip**
>
> Baguette slices • Crostini (page 180) • Breadsticks, store-bought or homemade (page 184) • Flatbread crisps • Cherry tomatoes • Green beans, prepared for dipping (see page 86) • Tiny new potatoes, cooked (see page 87) • Red bell pepper strips • Zucchini rounds

1 cup pitted and coarsely chopped Mediterranean green olives

2 teaspoons fresh lemon juice

1 teaspoon finely chopped fresh rosemary

1 teaspoon anchovy paste

1 garlic clove, crushed through a press

¼ teaspoon crushed hot red pepper

⅓ cup extra-virgin olive oil

1. Combine the olives, lemon juice, rosemary, anchovy paste, garlic, and crushed red pepper in a food processor and process until smooth. With the processor running, slowly add the oil and process until smooth. Transfer to a bowl, cover, and refrigerate to blend the flavors, at least 2 hours, or up to 1 week (if refrigerating for longer than 2 days, cover the tapenade with a thin film of olive oil)

2. Transfer to a serving bowl. Serve at room temperature, with a small knife for spreading.

Thai Peanut Dip

makes about 1¾ cups

MAKE-AHEAD: The dip can be made up to 2 days ahead.

I learned how to make peanut sauce at one of my first restaurant jobs, a place on Manhattan's Upper West Side with a Thai chef. Formerly considered exotic, it is now available in the Asian section of most supermarkets—but nothing beats homemade peanut sauce.

1 tablespoon vegetable oil

3 tablespoons finely chopped shallots

1 tablespoon shredded fresh ginger (use the large holes on a box grater)

2 garlic cloves, minced

1 teaspoon Madras-style curry powder

⅛ teaspoon crushed hot red pepper

½ cup smooth peanut butter (not natural-style)

1 cup canned low-sodium chicken broth, or use homemade stock

what to dip

Potato chips, store-bought or homemade (page 171 or 174) • Fried shrimp crackers (see page 169) • Broccoli or cauliflower florets, prepared for dipping (see page 85) • Carrot sticks • Celery sticks • Cucumber slices • Zucchini slices • Cooked chicken breast (skinless and boneless), cut into bite-sized cubes • Cooked shrimp (peeled and deveined)

3 tablespoons unsweetened coconut milk or heavy
  cream
1 tablespoon fresh lime juice
1 tablespoon Asian fish sauce (nam pla or nuoc cham)
  or soy sauce
1 teaspoon light brown sugar
Chopped fresh cilantro, including stems, for garnish

1.   Heat the oil in a medium heavy saucepan over medium
low-heat. Add the shallots, ginger, and garlic and cook, stirring often, until the shallots are golden, about 3 minutes.
Add the curry powder and red pepper and stir until fragrant, about 15 seconds.

2.   Whisk in the broth, peanut butter, coconut milk, lime
juice, fish sauce, and brown sugar. Bring to a simmer and
simmer over low heat to blend the flavors, about 3 minutes.
Transfer to a bowl and let cool, then cover and refrigerate
until chilled, at least 2 hours or up to 2 days (if the chilled
dip is too thick, thin with water or broth).

3.   Transfer to a serving bowl and sprinkle with the
cilantro. Serve at room temperature.

Tapenade

makes 1 cup

MAKE-AHEAD: The tapenade can be prepared up to 1 week ahead.

One of Provence's most delicious exports, tapenade is a compendium of Mediterranean flavors in each bite— olives, capers, anchovies, garlic, thyme, and red peppers. Tapenade is only as good as the olives, so it is important to use an imported variety, not the canned ones from California. Small Niçoise olives will have the most flavor, if you have the patience to pit them (they are actually quite soft, so it is easy to pinch them to remove the pits). The more readily available vinegar-cured Kalamata olives are different, but will certainly work.

> **what to dip**
>
> Baguette slices • Crostini (page 180) • Breadsticks, store-bought or homemade (page 184) • Flatbread crisps • Cherry tomatoes • Fennel bulb, cut into sticks • Tiny new potatoes, cooked (see page 87) • Red bell pepper strips • Zucchini rounds

1 cup pitted and coarsely
  chopped Mediterranean black olives
¼ cup nonpareil capers, drained and rinsed
1 teaspoon fresh lemon juice
1 teaspoon brandy
1 teaspoon Dijon mustard
1 teaspoon anchovy paste

1 teaspoon chopped fresh thyme
1 garlic clove, crushed through a press
Pinch of crushed hot red pepper
¼ cup extra-virgin olive oil

1.   Combine the olives, capers, lemon juice, brandy, mustard, anchovy paste, thyme, garlic, and red pepper in a food processor and puree. With the motor running, gradually add the oil and process until smooth. Transfer to a serving bowl, cover, and refrigerate to blend the flavors, at least 2 hours, or up to 1 week (if refrigerating for longer than 2 days, cover the tapenade with a thin film of olive oil).

2.   Serve at room temperature, with a small knife for spreading.

Herbed Yogurt Dip

makes about 1¾ cups

MAKE-AHEAD: The dip can be prepared up to 1 day ahead.

Some dips (and, let's face it, many other foods too) have a direct correlation between that high calorie count and fabulous flavor. Here's a change of pace that will make even the most fat-conscious guest at the party dive into the dip bowl, especially if served with reduced-fat chips or crudités. Drain the whey from yogurt, and the result is thick, creamy, and cheese-like—just the thing for turning into a dip.

> **what to dip**
>
> Potato chips, store-bought or homemade (page 171 or 174) • Broccoli and cauliflower florets, prepared for dipping (see page 85) • Carrot sticks • Celery sticks • Cherry tomatoes • Cucumber slices • Zucchini slices

1 quart plain low-fat (not nonfat) yogurt
2 scallions, white and green parts, finely chopped
2 tablespoons chopped fresh basil
2 tablespoons chopped fresh parsley
1 garlic clove, crushed through a press, optional
¼ teaspoon freshly ground black pepper
Salt to taste

1.   The day you will be serving the dip, line a sieve with paper towels and place over a large bowl (the bottom of the

sieve should clear the bottom of the bowl by a few inches). Spoon the yogurt into the sieve. Place another paper towel on the yogurt, and top with a saucer that fits into the sieve. Refrigerate until about 1¾ cups whey has drained from the yogurt and the yogurt has thickened into a soft cheese-like consistency, 2 to 4 hours. Discard the whey in the bowl.

2. Mix the yogurt cheese, scallions, basil, parsley, garlic, if using, and the pepper in a medium bowl. Season with the salt. Cover and refrigerate to blend the flavors, at least 2 hours, or up to 1 day.

3. Transfer to a serving bowl and serve chilled.

Basil Caesar Dip

makes about 2 cups

MAKE-AHEAD: The dip can be prepared up to 1 day ahead.

When researching an article on famous American foods, I was very surprised to learn that the first Caesar salad may have been more like a dip for Romaine lettuce leaves. This dip combines the flavors of Caesar salad dressing with basil, a very compatible herb.

1 cup mayonnaise
½ cup sour cream
½ cup freshly grated Parmesan or pecorino Romano
2 tablespoons chopped fresh basil, plus basil sprigs for garnish
1 tablespoon fresh lemon juice
½ teaspoon anchovy paste
1 garlic clove, crushed through a press

> ## what to dip
>
> Crostini (page 180) • Breadsticks, store-bought or homemade (page 184) • Frozen artichoke hearts, thawed • Asparagus spears, prepared for dipping (see page 84) • Cherry tomatoes • Cucumber slices • Mushroom caps • Romaine lettuce hearts

1. Mix the mayonnaise, sour cream, cheese, chopped basil, lemon juice, anchovy paste, and garlic in a medium bowl. Cover and refrigerate to blend the flavors, at least 1 hour, or up to 1 day.

2. Transfer the dip to a serving bowl and garnish with the basil sprigs. Serve chilled.

Spicy Salsas
and Dips

Salsa is the best friend a tortilla chip ever had. The word *salsa* means "sauce" in Spanish, showing that in Latin countries salsas are considered condiments for cooked food, not just for dipping tortilla chips. I'm glad that American ingenuity has made the most of the combination.

There are two basic kinds of salsa, raw and cooked. The

raw versions are chunky with bits of tomato, onion, garlic, and, of course, chiles, among other ingredients. The cooked versions are often pureed to yield smooth salsas with heightened flavors. Bean dip and guacamole are close relatives to salsas, and you'll find examples here. I have not included fruit salsas—which may be delicious served next to grilled salmon, but do nothing for a tortilla chip.

For information on chiles, see page 8.

Red Pumpkin-Seed Salsa

makes 1½ cups

MAKE-AHEAD: The salsa can be prepared up to 3 days ahead.

P*epián* is really a mole-related cooking sauce rather than a salsa. Nonetheless, whenever I make it, I find myself dipping tortillas in it. It has a few steps, but none of them are difficult, and the result is a rust-red salsa with complex flavors hinting of chocolate and fruit.

what to dip

Tortilla chips,
store-bought or
homemade (page 176)

2 ancho chiles, stemmed, split,
    and seeded
½ cup unsalted shelled pumpkin seeds
    (pepitas)
4 plum tomatoes
3 tablespoons olive oil
½ cup chopped white onion
2 garlic cloves, minced
1 canned chipotle chile en adobo, chopped
2 teaspoons honey
¼ teaspoon ground cinnamon
¼ teaspoon ground allspice
½ cup canned low-sodium chicken broth, or use
    homemade stock, as needed
Salt to taste

1. Heat a large skillet over medium-high heat. Place the chiles skin side down in the skillet and cook until they turn a deeper shade, and are more pliable, about 2 minutes. Transfer to a medium bowl, add hot water to cover, and put a saucer on top of the chiles to submerge them. Let stand until softened, about 20 minutes, then drain well.

2. Add the pumpkin seeds to the skillet and cook over medium heat, stirring often, until they have turned a deeper shade of olive, about 3 minutes. Transfer to a plate and let cool.

3. Position a broiler rack 6 inches from the source of heat and preheat the broiler. Place the tomatoes on the rack and broil, turning occasionally, until the skins are blackened and peeling, about 10 minutes. Peel the tomatoes, discarding the seeds.

4. Heat 1 tablespoon of the oil in a large skillet over medium heat. Add the onion and garlic and cook, stirring often, until softened, about 3 minutes. Remove from the heat.

5. Combine the drained chiles, toasted pumpkin seeds, tomatoes, onion and garlic, chipotle, honey, cinnamon, and allspice in a food processor or a blender. With the processor running, gradually add enough stock to make a thick puree.

6. Heat the remaining 2 tablespoons oil in the skillet over medium heat. Add the salsa (watch out for splatters) and bring to a boil. Cook, stirring often, until slightly reduced, about 3 minutes. Transfer to a medium bowl and let cool completely. Season with salt. (The dip can be prepared up to 3 days ahead, covered, and refrigerated; if the chilled dip is too thick, thin with water or broth.)

7. Transfer to a serving bowl and serve at room temperature.

Classic Tomato Salsa

makes about 2½ cups

MAKE-AHEAD: The salsa is best served within 2 hours, but it can be made up to 1 day ahead, covered, and refrigerated.

This is a well-balanced, not-too-hot raw salsa that will help make a bowl of tortilla chips disappear. Serve it soon after making it so the flavors stay distinct.

3 ripe large tomatoes
Salt
1 garlic clove
3 tablespoons finely chopped
   red or white onion
2 tablespoons fresh lime juice
1 jalapeño, seeded and minced
2 tablespoons chopped fresh cilantro

what to dip

Tortilla chips,
store-bought or
homemade (page 176)

1. Cut each tomato crosswise in half, and use your finger to poke out the seeds. Using a serrated knife, cut the tomatoes into ½-inch cubes. Toss the tomato cubes with ½ teaspoon salt in a colander. Let drain in the sink for at least 30 minutes, or up to 1 hour.

2. Finely chop the garlic. Sprinkle with a pinch of salt and continue to chop and smear the garlic on the work surface until it forms a paste.

3. Mix the tomatoes, onion, lime juice, jalapeño, cilantro, and garlic paste in a bowl. Let stand at room temperature for 20 minutes to blend the flavors.

4. Transfer the salsa to a serving bowl and serve.

GUACA SALSA   Just before serving, stir 1 ripe Hass avocado, pitted, peeled, and cut into ½-inch dice, into the salsa.

Tomatillo-Cilantro Salsa

makes about 3 cups

MAKE-AHEAD: The salsa can be prepared up to 1 day ahead.

The green salsa you put on your taco is not made from green tomatoes, but from tomatillos, a relative of the gooseberry (the papery husk on fresh tomatillos gives them away). You'll find them at grocers in Latino communities and specialty produce stores. Canned tomatillos are more common, but it is worth searching out the fresh ones. When boiling the tomatillos, take care not to cook them until they burst—it is better if they remain slightly raw.

what to dip

Tortilla chips, store-bought or homemade (page 176) • Cooked chicken breast (skinless and boneless) cut into bite-sized chunks • Cooked shrimp (peeled and deveined)

2 pounds tomatillos, husked
2 garlic cloves, crushed under the side of a knife and peeled
1 jalapeño, seeded and coarsely chopped
1 medium white onion, coarsely chopped
¼ cup packed fresh cilantro leaves, plus additional for garnish
2 tablespoons olive oil
Salt to taste

1.   Bring a medium saucepan of lightly salted water to a boil over high heat. Add the tomatillos and cook just until

tender but not falling apart, about 6 minutes. (If the tomatillos are different sizes, remove the smaller ones as they are done with a slotted spoon or skimmer.) Drain well.

2. With the processor running, drop the garlic and jalapeño through the feed tube of a food processor. Add the onion and cilantro and pulse until finely chopped. Add the tomatillos and pulse until chunky smooth, depending on your preference.

3. Heat the oil in a large skillet over medium-high heat. Add the salsa (watch out for splatters) and bring to a boil. Cook, stirring often, until slightly reduced, about 3 minutes. Transfer to a bowl and let cool completely.

4. Season the salsa with salt, cover tightly with plastic wrap, and refrigerate until chilled, at least 1 hour, or up to 1 day.

5. Transfer to a serving bowl and garnish with cilantro leaves. Serve chilled or at room temperature.

TOMATILLO-BASIL SALSA Substitute ¼ cup chopped basil for the cilantro. Garnish with a sprig of basil.

Grilled Corn and
Goat Cheese Salsa

makes about 4 cups

MAKE-AHEAD: The salsa can be prepared up to 8 hours ahead.

This colorful salsa celebrates the special time of year when corn and tomatoes are both in season. By the way, there's no need to soak corn before grilling, as some recipes direct. Yes, the husks will char, but that adds a wonderful smokiness to the kernels.

what to dip

Tortilla chips,
store-bought or
homemade (page 176) •
Corn chips

4 ears corn (unhusked)
2 large beefsteak tomatoes,
    seeded and cut into ½-inch dice
½ teaspoon salt, plus more to taste
2 scallions, white and green parts, chopped
1 red or green jalapeño, seeded and minced
2 tablespoons chopped fresh cilantro
1 garlic clove, crushed through a press
3 ounces rindless goat cheese, crumbled

1. Build a charcoal fire in a outdoor grill and let burn until the coals are covered with white ash. Or preheat a gas grill on High.

2. Place the corn on the grill, cover, and grill, turning occasionally, until the husks are charred, about 20 minutes. Take care not to burn the husks down to the kernels. Remove from the grill and let cool until easy to handle.

3. Meanwhile, place the tomatoes in a colander and toss with the ½ teaspoon salt. Let stand in the sink or a larger bowl to drain off excess liquid, about 30 minutes.

4. Remove and discard the husks and silk from the ears. Trim the bottom of each ear so it can be held upright, stand the ear on end, and cut the kernels from the cob.

5. Mix the corn, tomatoes, scallions, jalapeño, cilantro, and garlic in a medium bowl. Stir in about half of the cheese, reserving the rest for garnish. Season with salt. Cover and refrigerate to blend the flavors at least 1 hour, or up to 1 day.

6. Transfer to a serving bowl. Garnish with the reserved cheese and serve chilled or at room temperature.

Ranchero Salsa

makes 2½ cups

MAKE-AHEAD: The salsa can be prepared up to 1 day ahead.

The preferred salsa of the Mexican ranchers in the north, this cooked salsa usually covers a plate of huevos rancheros. It makes a great dip for tortilla chips too.

what to dip

Tortilla chips, store-bought or homemade (page 176) • Corn chips

2 tablespoons olive oil
1 medium onion, chopped
2 garlic cloves, minced
2 tablespoons chopped fresh
   cilantro, plus more for
   garnish
1 teaspoon toasted and ground cumin seeds
   (see page 10)
½ teaspoon dried oregano
One 14½-ounce can chopped tomatoes in juice
3 mild chiles, such as Anaheim, New Mexico, or
   poblano, roasted (see page 9), peeled, seeded, and
   chopped
Salt to taste

1.   Heat the oil in a medium skillet over medium heat. Add the onion and cook, stirring occasionally, until softened, about 3 minutes. Add the garlic and cook until fragrant, about 1 minute. Stir in the cilantro, cumin, and oregano.

Add the tomatoes, with their juice, and the chiles. Bring to a boil and cook until the salsa is thickened, about 5 minutes.

2.   Transfer to a food processor and pulse until chunky. Season with salt. Transfer to a serving bowl and cool completely. (The salsa can be prepared up to 1 day ahead, cooled, covered, and refrigerated.)

3.   Garnish with cilantro and serve at room temperature.

Red Flame Salsa

makes about 3 cups

MAKE-AHEAD: The salsa can be prepared up to 2 days ahead.

Ancho chiles give this salsa its moderately high heat level and deep red color. If you wish, add 1 cup fresh or frozen corn kernels or canned beans to the salsa to provide extra substance.

what to dip

Tortilla chips,
store-bought or
homemade (page 176)

4 ancho chiles, stemmed, split
    and seeded
1 tablespoon olive oil
1 medium onion, chopped
2 garlic cloves, minced
1 jalapeño, seeded and minced
One 14½-ounce can tomatoes in juice, drained, juice
    reserved
1 tablespoon fresh lime juice
Salt to taste

1. Heat a large skillet over medium-high heat. Place the chiles skin side down in the skillet and cook until they are a deeper shade and more pliable, about 2 minutes. Transfer to a medium bowl, add enough hot water to cover, and put a saucer on top of the chiles to submerge them. Let stand until softened, about 20 minutes, then drain well.

2. Heat the oil in a medium skillet over medium heat. Add the onion, jalapeño, and garlic and cook, stirring often, until the onion softens, about 3 minutes. Remove from the heat.

3. Combine the drained tomatoes and chiles in a blender. Puree, adding enough of the reserved tomato juice to reach the desired thickness. Transfer to a medium bowl, stir in the onion mixture, and season with salt. Let cool to room temperature. (The dip can be prepared up to 2 days ahead, covered, and refrigerated.)

4. Transfer to a serving bowl and serve at room temperature.

Three-Bean Salsa

makes 6 cups

MAKE-AHEAD: The salsa can be prepared up to 1 day ahead.

Looking for a bean salsa to serve a crowd? Try this colorful mix of black, pinto, and garbanzo beans, accented with tomatoes, chiles, and onion. If you want to stretch it further, add 2 cups shredded sharp Cheddar cheese.

what to dip

Tortilla chips, store-bought or homemade (page 176) • Corn chips

One 15½- to 19-ounce can black
   beans, drained and rinsed
One 15½- to 19-ounce can pinto
   beans, drained and rinsed
One 15½- to 19-ounce can garbanzo beans
   (chickpeas), drained and rinsed
2 ripe beefsteak tomatoes, preferably 1 red and
   1 yellow, seeded and cut into ½-inch dice
1 red bell pepper, roasted (see page 12), peeled, seeded,
   and diced
1 mild chile, such as Anaheim or poblano, or green bell
   pepper, roasted (see page 9 or page 12), peeled,
   seeded, and diced
1 jalapeño, seeded and minced
1 medium red onion, finely chopped
2 garlic cloves, crushed through a press
3 tablespoons chopped fresh oregano

2 tablespoons red wine vinegar
2 tablespoons extra-virgin olive oil
Salt to taste

1.   Mix the black beans, pinto beans, garbanzo beans, tomatoes, red pepper, chile, jalapeño, onion, garlic, oregano, vinegar, and oil in a large bowl.

2.   Transfer half of the salsa to a food processor and pulse until fairly smooth. Stir back into the bowl. Season with salt. Cover and refrigerate to blend the flavors, at least 1 hour, or up to 1 day.

3.   Transfer to a serving bowl and serve chilled or at room temperature.

Black Bean and Bacon Dip

makes 5 cups

MAKE-AHEAD: The dip can be prepared up to 2 days ahead.

Here's a versatile bean dip that can be served hot or cold. By varying the amount of liquid, you can make it as thick or thin as you like.

6 bacon slices
1 medium onion, chopped
1 small green bell pepper, cored,
    seeded, and chopped
1 jalapeño, seeded and minced
1 garlic clove, minced
1 teaspoon ground cumin
1 teaspoon dried oregano
One 14½-ounce can diced tomatoes in juice
Two 15½- to 19-ounce cans black beans, drained,
    liquid reserved
Salt and freshly ground black pepper to taste
Sour cream for garnish

> **what to dip**
>
> Tortilla chips,
> store-bought or
> homemade (page 176) •
> Corn chips

1.   Cook the bacon in a large skillet over medium heat until crisp and browned, about 5 minutes. Using a slotted spatula, transfer the bacon to paper towels to drain and cool.

2.   Pour out all but 2 tablespoons of the bacon fat from the skillet and return to medium heat. Add the onion, green

pepper, and jalapeño. Cook, stirring often, until softened, about 6 minutes. Add the garlic and stir until fragrant, about 1 minute. Stir in the cumin and oregano. Add the tomatoes with their juice and the beans and bring to a simmer. Cook, stirring often, until the beans are heated through, about 10 minutes.

3. Chop the bacon. Transfer half of the bean mixture to a food processor and process until smooth. Stir back into the skillet, along with the bacon. If desired, thin with some of the reserved canned bean liquid. Season with salt and pepper. Cover and refrigerate until chilled, at least 2 hours, or up to 2 days.

4. Transfer to a serving dish and top with a large dollop of sour cream. Serve chilled.

HOT BLACK BEAN AND BACON DIP   The dip can also be served hot. Heat 2 tablespoons reserved bacon fat or vegetable oil in a large nonstick skillet over medium heat. Add the prepared dip and cook, stirring often, until heated through, about 5 minutes.

Smoky Chorizo and Chipotle Dip

makes about 2½ cups

MAKE-AHEAD: The dip can be prepared up to 2 days ahead.

This dip gets a double dose of smoky flavor from chorizo sausage and chipotle chiles en adobo. Use smoked chorizo sausage, which is hard and can be diced. Fresh chorizo which is like a very spicy bulk sausage, isn't right for this dip. You'll find chorizo at Latino grocers and larger supermarkets.

what to dip

Tortilla chips, store-bought or homemade (page 176) • Corn chips

1 tablespoon olive oil
4 ounces smoked chorizo sausage, finely chopped
1 medium onion, chopped
1 small red bell pepper, cored, seeded, and chopped
1 garlic clove, minced
½ teaspoon dried oregano
½ teaspoon ground cumin
Two 15½- to 19-ounce cans pinto beans
1 canned chile chipotle en adobo, minced
Salt to taste
½ cup sour cream for garnish
Chopped fresh cilantro for garnish

1. Combine the chorizo and oil in a medium skillet and cook over medium heat, stirring often, until the chorizo is browned, about 7 minutes. Using a slotted spoon, transfer the chorizo to paper towels, leaving the fat in the pan.

2. Add the onion and red pepper to the skillet. Cook, stirring often, until the pepper is tender, about 6 minutes. Add the garlic, oregano, and cumin and stir until the garlic is fragrant, about 1 minute. Add the beans with their liquid and the chipotle pepper and bring to a simmer, stirring often. Reduce the heat to low and simmer for 5 minutes.

3. Transfer 1 cup of the bean mixture to a food processor and puree. Stir back into the skillet, along with the chorizo. Transfer to a medium bowl and let cool. Season with salt, cover, and refrigerate until chilled, at least 2 hours, or up to 2 days. (If the chilled dip is too thick, thin with water or broth.)

4. Transfer to a serving bowl. Top with the sour cream and sprinkle with cilantro. Serve chilled or at room temperature.

Texas Caviar

makes about 6 cups

MAKE-AHEAD: The dip can be prepared up to 2 days ahead.

Ersatz caviar, dip or spread made from small or chopped ingredients that somewhat resemble tiny grains of salted fish eggs, is an entire dip sub-category. In this case, the black-eyed peas play the role of caviar (although those would be Texas-sized fish)! I don't think I've ever been to a party in Texas that hasn't served up this kissin' cousin to bean salsa. For tenderfoot-mild caviar with a gentle kick, use just one jalapeño. If you want a spicier dip, substitute 2 tablespoons or more chopped pickled jalapeños, and add a bit of the pickling juice to the dip to taste.

what to dip

Tortilla chips, store-bought or homemade (page 176) • Corn chips

Three 15½- to 19-ounce cans black-eyed peas, drained and rinsed

½ cup chopped (¼-inch dice) sweet onion, such as Texas Sweet or Vidalia

½ cup chopped (¼-inch dice) red bell pepper

½ cup chopped (¼-inch dice) celery

2 jalapeños, seeded and minced

3 tablespoons cider vinegar

½ teaspoon sugar

2 garlic cloves, crushed through a press
½ cup olive oil
Salt and freshly ground black pepper to taste
3 tablespoons chopped fresh cilantro (optional)

1. Mix the black eye peas, onion, red pepper, celery, and jalapeños in a large bowl.

2. Whisk the vinegar, sugar, and garlic in small bowl. Gradually whisk in the oil. Stir into the beans. Season with salt and pepper. Cover and refrigerate for at least 2 hours, or up to 2 days.

3. Just before serving, stir in the cilantro, if using. Transfer to a serving bowl and serve chilled or at room temperature.

TEXAS CAVIAR WITH BACON   Just before serving, add 8 bacon slices, cooked until crisp, drained and finely chopped, to the caviar.

Ultimate Tex-Mex Layered Dip

makes 12 to 16 servings

MAKE-AHEAD: The dip can be prepared up to 8 hours ahead.

I am a huge fan of layered dip, which is one of those recipes that no one seems to know exactly where it came from, although it may have originated in Fort Worth in the early eighties. The original (see the variation) starts with canned refried beans. As I am always looking to make a good thing better, I don't mind taking a little extra time to make this magnificent from-scratch version.

> **what to dip**
>
> Tortilla chips, store-bought or homemade (page 176) • Corn chips

Black Bean and Bacon Dip (page 68)
The Best Guacamole (page 76)
One 1-pint container sour cream
Classic Tomato Salsa (page 56)
1 cup (4 ounces) crumbled feta cheese

1.   Spread the bean dip in a thick layer on a serving platter. Spread with the guacamole, then with the sour cream, being sure to completely cover the guacamole. Top with a layer of the salsa, then sprinkle with the cheese. Cover loosely with plastic wrap and refrigerate until chilled, at least 1 hour, or up to 8 hours.

2. Serve chilled.

CLASSIC SEVEN-LAYER DIP   Spread two 15½-ounce cans refried beans in a thick layer on a platter. Mash 3 ripe Hass avocados, pitted and peeled, with 3 tablespoons fresh lemon juice and season with salt. Spread over the beans. Mix 1½ cups sour cream with one 1¼-ounce envelope taco seasoning mix, and spread over the avocado. Top with, in the following order, two 2¼-ounce cans chopped black olives, drained; 2 pickled or fresh jalapeños, cut into thin rounds; 4 scallions, white and green parts chopped; 3 ripe plum tomatoes, chopped; and 2 cups (8 ounces) shredded sharp Cheddar. Cover, chill, and serve as above.

The Best Guacamole

makes about 2½ cups

MAKE-AHEAD: Guacamole is best served right after a 30-minute rest, but it can be made ahead up to 1 day ahead.

I once spent a summer session of college in Guadalajara, where my Spanish didn't improve, but I sure got a lot of great recipes. My host family taught me all about guacamole: Never make guacamole in a blender or food processor. It is supposed to be chunky, not smooth. Even more important is the right avocado. The Hass variety, with pebbly black skin, is far superior in flavor and texture to the kind with shiny green skin. Finally when seasoning, be bold with the salt, as avocados need more than you might think.

what to dip

Tortilla chips, store-bought or homemade (page 176) • Corn chips

3 ripe Hass avocados, pitted, peeled, and chopped
⅓ cup chopped onion, preferably white onion
2 tablespoons chopped fresh cilantro, plus more for
    garnish, optional
2 tablespoons fresh lime juice
1 jalapeño, seeded and minced
Salt
1 garlic clove
1 ripe plum tomato, seeded and cut into ½-inch dice

1. Using a potato masher or large fork, mash the avocados with the onion, cilantro, if using, lime juice, and jalapeño in a medium bowl.

2. Finely chop the garlic. Sprinkle with a pinch of salt, and chop and smear the garlic on the work surface until it forms a paste. Stir into the mashed avocados, along with the tomatoes. Season with a generous amount of salt. Let stand at room temperature for 30 minutes to blend the flavors. (To serve later, press a piece of plastic wrap directly on the surface of the guacamole and refrigerate for up to 1 day; stir well before serving.

3. Transfer to a serving bowl, garnish with cilantro, if desired, and serve.

Creamy Avocado Dip

makes 2 cups

MAKE-AHEAD: The dip can be prepared up to 1 day ahead.

Chunky guacamole is, of course, the most authentic way to go, especially when serving it with tortilla chips. But there are times when a thick but creamy avocado dip would work better (think of crudités or potato chips), and that's when to use this recipe. I learned it during my student days in Mexico, when my landlady served it as a table sauce.

what to dip

Tortilla chips, store-bought or homemade (page 176) • Carrot sticks • Celery sticks • Cherry tomatoes • Cucumber slices • Zucchini slices

2 ripe Hass avocados, pitted and
    peeled
½ cup Mexican crema
    (see Note) or sour cream
1 tablespoon grated onion (use the large holes of a box
    grater)
2 teaspoons seeded and minced jalapeño
1 garlic clove, crushed through a press
Salt to taste
Chopped tomatoes for garnish
Chopped fresh cilantro for garnish

1. Combine the avocados, crema, onion, jalapeño, and garlic in a food processor and process until smooth. Season

with salt (avocados tend to take a good amount of salt, so don't be shy).

2. Transfer to a bowl and press a piece of plastic wrap directly on the dip surface to keep out air and discourage discoloring. Cover tightly and refrigerate until chilled, at least 2 hours, or up to 1 day.

3. Stir the dip well. Garnish with chopped tomatoes and cilantro, and serve chilled.

NOTE: Crema is Mexican sour cream, slightly more fluid than the American version. It can be found in the dairy section of Latino grocers.

Diane's Supreme Avocado Dip

makes about 3 cups

MAKE-AHEAD: The dip can be prepared up to 5 hours ahead. The chopped toppings can also be prepared up to 5 hours ahead, individually wrapped, and refrigerated, but garnish the dip just before serving.

My friend and colleague Diane Phillips and I love to swap recipes. She's known at cooking schools across the country for her hassle-free approach to cooking, and, like many busy cooks, she is not afraid to use convenience foods. Whenever I serve this dip, a mild-mannered guacamole with ranch dressing tendencies, my guests love it.

what to dip

Tortilla chips, store-bought or homemade (page 176)

4 ripe Hass avocados, pitted and peeled
2 tablespoons fresh lime juice
Salt to taste
1½ cups sour cream
1 cup mayonnaise
One 1-ounce envelope ranch-style dressing and dip mix

TOPPINGS
3 plum tomatoes, seeded and chopped
3 scallions, white and green parts, chopped
½ cup shredded sharp Cheddar

One 2¼-ounce can chopped ripe olives, drained
¼ cup drained and chopped pickled jalapeños
2 tablespoons chopped fresh cilantro

1. Mash the avocados and lime juice in a medium bowl until smooth. Season lightly with salt (the next layer is salty and will season the avocados). Spread the avocados in a thick layer on a round or oval platter.

2. Stir the sour cream, mayonnaise, and dressing mix in a small bowl, blending well. Spread over the avocados, being sure to cover them completely. Cover loosely with plastic wrap and refrigerate until chilled, about 1 hour. (The dip can be prepared to this point up to 5 hours ahead.)

3. Just before serving, arrange a ring of the tomatoes around the edge of the dip. Make progressively smaller rings of the scallions, cheese, olives, and jalapeños, on the dip, ending with the cilantro in the center. Serve immediately.

Vegging
Out

Here's a statistic I'd like to know: How many "crudités and dip" are served every day? This happy combination seems right for every occasion, from an after-work celebration to a fancy cocktail party. But while the assortment of vegetables may stay the same, the choice of dip sets the mood.

Most of the recipes in this chapter feature the flavors

and textures of roasted, pureed, and chopped vegetables. One of the advantages of vegetable-based dips is that most of them don't contain ingredients (such as meat and eggs) that restrict the length of their "safe" serving time to two hours. Other recipes, such as Herb-Garlic Vinaigrette, Tahini-Carrot Dip, and Miso-Ginger Dip are perfect for serving with vegetables. Of course, the selection isn't limited to the recipes in this chapter—many favorite dips are crossovers into this category.

Vegetables for Dipping

Crudités, by definition, means raw vegetables. However, some vegetables (such as broccoli, cauliflower, and green beans) benefit from a quick boiling to brighten their color and soften their crunch. If you are parcooking a variety of vegetables, you don't need to boil a pan of fresh water every time. Start with the vegetables with the mildest flavor (carrots) and work your way up to the more strongly flavored (broccoli and cauliflower). Certain other vegetables, such as potatoes, should be thoroughly cooked. In either case, wrap the vegetables in paper towels (to absorb excess moisture and keep them crisp) and store in the refrigerator in ziptight plastic bags.

When you're in a hurry and want to reduce the time needed to cut up vegetables, stop by the salad bar in your market to see what's displayed that could be dipped.

To arrange the crudités, place vegetables with contrasting colors and shapes next to each other to increase eye appeal.

Here are some serving suggestions for the most popular vegetables for dipping.

FRESH BABY ARTICHOKES   These are a must for aïoli and bagna cauda. To trim baby artichokes, snap back all of the tough outer leaves until you reach the cone of pale, tender leaves. Using a small sharp knife, cut off the tip of the cone, about ½ inch from the top. Trim off all of the dark green skin from the base and the stem, if attached. Rub the cut surfaces all over with a lemon half, and drop into a bowl of water to which the juice of the other half of the lemon has been added.

To cook the artichokes, bring a large saucepan of lightly salted water to a boil over high head. Drain the artichokes, add to the water, and reduce the heat to medium. Cover and cook until the artichokes are tender when pierced with the tip of a knife, about 20 minutes. Drain and rinse under cold water. Pat dry. Wrap in paper towels and store in a ziptight bag in the refrigerator for up to 1 day. Before serving, cut each artichoke in half lengthwise, if desired.

Thawed frozen artichoke hearts make great dippers. Rinse the artichokes well in a colander under cold water, drain, and pat completely dry with paper towels. Serve either artichoke with toothpicks to hold them during dipping.

ASPARAGUS   Bend each asparagus spear to break off the thick end. Cook in a large saucepan of lightly salted water just until crisp-tender, about 2 minutes, depending on the thickness of the asparagus; do not overcook. Drain, rinse well under cold water, and drain again. Spread out the spears on paper towels and pat completely dry. Wrap in fresh paper towels and refrigerate in ziptight plastic bags for up to 1 day.

BROCCOLI   Cut broccoli florets into bite-sized pieces. If you wish, peel the stems and cut crosswise into ¼-inch-thick slices (no need to peel the stems of the florets, as the skin is more tender). Cook in a large saucepan of lightly salted water just until the color brightens, about 1 minute; do not overcook. Drain, rinse under cold water, and drain well, shaking the colander to remove as much water as possible. Spread on paper towels and pat completely dry. Wrap in fresh paper towels and refrigerate in ziptight plastic bags for up to 1 day.

CARROTS   Peel carrots and cut into 1-inch-thick sticks. Or use whole "baby-cut" carrots. Carrot sticks can be served raw, but baby carrots sometimes look tired. If necessary, cook baby carrots in a large saucepan of lightly salted water just until the color brightens, about 1 minute. Rinse well under cold water to stop the cooking, drain, and pat completely dry with paper towels. In either case, wrap the carrots in paper towels and refrigerate in a ziptight plastic bag for up to 1 day.

CAULIFLOWER   See Broccoli.

CELERY   Some supermarkets now carry celery sticks for dipping, but I prefer to cut my own. Celery sticks need no special preparation. To keep crisp, wrap in moistened paper towels and refrigerate in a ziptight plastic bag for up to 1 day.

CHERRY TOMATOES   The classic cherry tomato is best for dipping; try to find tomatoes that still have the stem attached to use as a handle. The new sweet varieties, sometimes called grape tomatoes, are tasty but a little too small to serve with dips. Rinse the tomatoes, drain, and pat dry. Refrigerate in ziptight plastic bags for up to 3 days.

CUCUMBERS   Seedless (English) cucumbers are the best variety for dipping, as their skin is edible. If using regular cucumbers, peel off the waxy skin. Cucumbers are easiest to handle if cut into ¼-inch-thick rounds. A mandoline or plastic vegetable slicer will give uniform slices. Or cut the cucumber into 2- to 3-inch long, ½-inch-thick sticks. Wrap in paper towels and refrigerate in ziptight plastic bags for up to 1 day.

FENNEL BULB   Cut off the fronds and the stalks, if still attached. Cut the fennel bulb lengthwise in half, and cut out the thick core from each half in a wedge. Cut lengthwise into ½-inch-thick slices, then cut them to separate the layers into sticks. If you wish, trim the fennel stalks and cut them lengthwise into sticks. Wrap in paper towels and refrigerate in ziptight plastic bags for up to 1 day.

GREEN BEANS   Trim the ends. Cook in a large saucepan of lightly salted water just until the color brightens, about 1 minute; do not overcook. Drain, rinse under cold water, and drain again. Pat dry with paper towels. Wrap in paper towels and refrigerate in ziptight plastic bags for up to 1 day.

MUSHROOMS   Some cooks advise against rinsing mushrooms, but I like to be sure to remove all of the grit without resorting to brushing them clean one by one. Just take care not to soak the mushrooms in the water, and you'll be fine. Small white button mushrooms with the stems attached are best for dipping, but you can cut washed large mushrooms into halves or quarters if you wish. Place the mushrooms in a colander and rinse quickly under cold running water, agitating the mushrooms so they all are rinsed by the stream. Drain well and pat dry with paper towels. Wrap in fresh paper towels and refrigerate in ziptight bags for up to 8 hours.

POTATOES   Look for marble-sized tiny new potatoes at specialty markets. Scrub them well, but don't peel them. Cook in a large saucepan of lightly salted water until tender when pierced with the tip of a small knife, about 15 minutes. Drain and rinse under cold running water to stop the cooking. Cool completely. Wrap in paper towels and refrigerate in ziptight plastic bags.

RADISHES   Use bunched radishes for the freshest flavor and most attractive appearance. Scrub well and trim, leaving a small amount of the stem attached to act as a handle. To crisp, refrigerate in a bowl of ice water for at least 1 hour, or up to 1 day. Drain well and pat dry with paper towels.

SNAP PEAS AND SNOW PEAS   Trim the peas. Cook in a large saucepan of lightly salted water just until the color brightens, about 30 seconds; do not overcook. Drain and rinse under cold water. Pat completely dry on paper towels. Wrap in fresh paper towels and refrigerate in ziptight plastic bags for up to 8 hours (these don't keep well for long).

BELL PEPPERS   Use red, yellow, and/or green peppers. Slice off the top and bottom; slice down one side, and remove the ribs and seeds. Cut lengthwise into ¼-inch-thick strips. Wrap in paper towels and refrigerate in ziptight plastic bags for up to 1 day.

ZUCCHINI AND YELLOW SQUASH   Scrub well under cold water to remove surface grit. Slice (use a mandoline or plastic vegetable slicer if you have one) into ¼-inch-thick rounds. Or cut into ½-inch-thick sticks. Wrap in paper towels and refrigerate in ziptight plastic bags for up to 1 day.

Roasted Ratatouille

makes about 6 cups

MAKE-AHEAD: The ratatouille can be prepared up to 3 days ahead.

Ratatouille, a mélange of vegetables in an herbed tomato sauce, is one of the most versatile vegetable stews in the French cuisine repertoire; it also makes a wonderful dip. The traditional Niçoise cooking method involves lots of sautéing of the eggplant, zucchini, red pepper, and other vegetables—tedious and not especially necessary to the ratatouille's success. Some time ago, as a timesaving measure, I began roasting the most obvious ingredients, a process that not only cut down on the work, but also enhances the flavor.

> **what to dip**
>
> Fresh baguette slices •
> Bruschetta (page 182) •
> Crostini (page 180) •
> Flatbread crisps

1 large eggplant (2¼ pounds), cut into 1-inch cubes
2 medium zucchini, trimmed and cut into ¾-inch cubes
2 large red bell peppers, cored, stemmed, seeded, and cut into ¾-inch pieces
5 tablespoons extra-virgin olive oil
Salt and freshly ground black pepper to taste
2 large onions, chopped
3 garlic cloves, minced

One 28-ounce can tomatoes in juice, drained, juice
  reserved, and coarsely chopped
1 tablespoon herbes de Provence (see Note)
2 tablespoons chopped fresh parsley, plus more for
  garnish

1. Position a rack in the top third of the oven and preheat
the oven to 450°F.

2. Toss the eggplant, zucchini, and red pepper with 3
tablespoons of the oil in a large roasting pan. Season with
salt and pepper. Roast, stirring occasionally, until the vegetables are tender, about 45 minutes.

3. Meanwhile, heat the remaining 2 tablespoons oil in a
large saucepan over medium heat. Add the onions and
cook, stirring often, until tender, about 5 minutes. Add the
garlic and stir until fragrant, about 1 minute. Stir in the
tomatoes with their juice and the herbes de Provence. Bring
to a simmer. Reduce the heat to medium-low and simmer,
stirring often, until the juices are almost completely evaporated and the sauce is thick, about 30 minutes

4. Stir the roasted vegetables and parsley into the sauce.
Simmer for 5 minutes. Transfer to a food processor and
pulse to make a thick, chunky dip. Scrape into a bowl and
let cool.

5. Season the dip with salt and pepper. Cover tightly with plastic wrap and refrigerate until chilled, at least 2 hours, or up to 3 days.

6. Transfer to a serving bowl. Sprinkle the top with the parsley, and serve chilled or at room temperature.

NOTE: Herbes de Provence is a blend of Provençal herbs such as thyme, savory, and lavender. It is available at specialty food stores and many supermarkets. If necessary, substitute 1 teaspoon each dried basil, thyme, and rosemary.

Steve's Roasted Artichoke and Ricotta Dip

makes 3 cups

MAKE-AHEAD: The dip can be prepared up to 2 days ahead.

My friend Steve Evasew, one of the best caterers in Manhattan, is a constant source of recipe inspiration. Here's a classy artichoke dip that he has been serving at parties for years. Roasting works wonders with artichokes, and gives them an elusive flavor. The artichoke trimming may seem a chore at first, but it's easy to master.

> **what to dip**
>
> Bruschetta (page 182) •
> Crostini (page 180) •
> Flatbread crisps •
> Carrot sticks • Celery
> sticks • Cherry
> tomatoes • Cucumber
> slices • Zucchini slices

1 lemon, cut in half
4 medium (10-ounce)
    artichokes, preferably with
    stems attached
2 tablespoons extra-virgin olive oil
2 large heads garlic, roasted (see page 10)
2 cups ricotta cheese
½ cup freshly grated Parmesan cheese
1 medium red bell pepper, roasted (see page 12),
    peeled, seeded, and cut into ¼-inch dice
2 tablespoons chopped fresh basil
Salt to taste
Crushed hot red pepper to taste

1.   Position a rack in the center of the oven and preheat the oven to 400°F. Lightly grease a roasting pan with olive oil.

2.   Squeeze the juice from the lemon into a bowl filled with 1 quart water and drop the rinds into the bowl. One at a time, trim the artichokes: Snap off the thick dark green leaves until you reach the inner core of thin light green leaves; discard the leaves. Using a sharp knife, cut off the core of leaves where it meets the heart (there is often an indentation at this point), to reveal the heart. Using a dessert spoon, scoop out the fuzzy choke. Using a sharp paring knife, trim off all the dark green skin from the artichoke heart and stem. Place the trimmed artichoke hearts in the lemon water as you go.

3.   Drain the artichokes and toss with the oil in the roasting pan. Add ¼ cup hot water and cover tightly with aluminum foil. Roast for 20 minutes. Remove the foil and continue roasting until the artichokes are tinged with gold and tender when pierced with a knife, 15 to 20 minutes. Let the artichokes cool, then cut into ½-inch cubes.

4.   Squeeze the softened flesh from the garlic skins into a medium bowl. Mash the garlic with a fork. Stir in the chopped artichokes, ricotta, Parmesan, bell pepper, and basil. Season with salt and red pepper flakes. Cover tightly and refrigerate until chilled, at least 1 hour, or up to 2 days.

5.   Transfer to a serving bowl and serve chilled.

Broccoli and Cheddar Dip

makes about 3½ cups

MAKE-AHEAD: The dip can be prepared up to 1 day ahead.

This is a gilded-lily version of the hot dip classic, for which I provide a recipe as a "no-brainer" variation. If you prefer, use either cauliflower or broccoflower as a substitute for the broccoli. Other sharp semi-hard cheeses, such as Gruyère, work well too.

> **what to dip**
>
> Baguette slices • Broccoli and cauliflower florets, prepared for dipping (see page 85) • Carrot sticks • Celery sticks • Cherry tomatoes • Cucumber slices • Tiny new potatoes, cooked (see page 87) • Zucchini slices

2 cups coarsely chopped broccoli florets
1 cup milk
1 cup canned low-sodium chicken broth
3 tablespoons unsalted butter
½ cup finely chopped onion
1 medium celery rib, finely chopped
2 tablespoons dry sherry
¼ cup all-purpose flour
1½ cups (6 ounces) shredded extra-sharp Cheddar
Freshly ground black pepper to taste

1. Bring a medium saucepan of lightly salted water to a boil over high heat. Add the broccoli and cook until tender, about 5 minutes. Drain and rinse under cold water.

2. Heat the milk and broth until steaming in a small saucepan over low heat or in a microwave.

3. Meanwhile, melt the butter in a heavy medium saucepan over medium heat. Add the onion and celery and cook until the onion is translucent, about 3 minutes. Add the sherry and cook until it has evaporated, about 30 seconds. Stir in the flour. Whisk in the hot milk and bring to a simmer. Reduce the heat to low and simmer uncovered, whisking occasionally, until smooth and thickened and no raw flour taste remains, about 10 minutes.

4. Stir in the cheese until melted, then stir in the broccoli. Season with pepper. (The dip can be prepared up to 1 day ahead, cooled, covered, and refrigerated. Reheat gently in a double boiler over simmering water, whisking often.)

5. Transfer to a heatproof serving dish and serve hot.

CLASSIC BROCCOLI AND CHEESE DIP   Melt 1 pound pasteurized processed cheese spread, cut into cubes, in a medium saucepan over low heat. Add one 10-ounce package chopped broccoli, thawed and squeezed well to remove excess water, and 1 small onion, shredded on the large holes of a box grater. Heat through.

Roasted Carrot and Peanut Spread

makes 3 cups

MAKE-AHEAD: The spread can be prepared up to 3 days ahead.

The inspiration came from a menu at a pita sandwich restaurant that served carrot hummus, which turned out to be garbanzo bean puree with shredded carrots. My version is all-carrot, with an unusual blend of flavors that promises to be a subject of conversation.

what to spread

Pita bread wedges •
Pita Toasts (page 179) •
Crostini (page 180) •
Flatbread crisps

3 pounds carrots, peeled and
cut into 1-inch chunks
⅔ cup extra-virgin olive oil, or as needed
3 scallions, white and green parts, finely chopped, plus
more for garnish
3 tablespoons creamy peanut butter
2 tablespoons fresh lime juice
1 teaspoon ground cumin, preferably ground toasted
seeds (see page 10)
1 garlic clove, crushed through a press
⅛ teaspoon ground hot red (cayenne) pepper
Salt to taste
Chopped roasted peanuts for garnish

1.   Position a rack in the top third of the oven and preheat the oven to 400°F. Lightly oil a jelly-roll pan.

2.   Toss the carrots with 1 tablespoon of the oil on the pan, and spread them out. Add ¼ cup hot water and cover tightly with foil. Roast for 20 minutes. Remove the foil and continue roasting until the carrots are tender and tinged with brown (some may be caramelized—that's fine), 20 to 30 minutes longer.

3.   Transfer the carrots to a food processor, add the scallions, peanut butter, lime juice, cumin, garlic, and ground red pepper, and pulse to combine. With the processor running, add enough of the remaining oil to make a thick dip. Season with salt. Transfer to a medium bowl and cover tightly. Refrigerate to blend the flavors, at least 1 hour, or up to 3 days.

4.   Transfer to a serving bowl, top with the peanuts and scallions, and serve at room temperature.

Curried Vegetable Dip

makes 3 cups

MAKE-AHEAD: The dip can be prepared up to 2 days ahead.

This gently spiced dip is a natural for crudités. Play up
the Indian connection by also serving pappadums and
other Far Eastern breadstuffs.

One 12-ounce container
   whipped cream cheese
½ cup plain yogurt, plus more if
   needed
2 tablespoons Major Grey's
   chutney (see Note)
2 teaspoons Madras-style curry
   powder
Pinch of ground hot red
   (cayenne) pepper
1 small carrot, finely chopped
1 small celery rib, finely
   chopped
2 scallions, white and green
   parts, finely chopped
1 garlic clove, crushed through a press
Salt to taste
Chopped fresh cilantro for garnish

> **what to dip**
>
> Pappadums (see page
> 168) • Indian bread,
> such as naan, cut into
> bite-sized pieces •
> Flatbread crisps •
> Broccoli and
> cauliflower florets,
> prepared for dipping
> (see page 85) • Carrot
> sticks • Celery sticks •
> Cherry tomatoes •
> Cucumber slices •
> Zucchini slices

1. Mash the cream cheese, yogurt, chutney, curry powder,
and red pepper in a medium bowl until blended. Mix in the

carrot, celery, scallions, and garlic. Season with salt. Cover tightly and refrigerate until chilled, at least 2 hours, or up to 2 days.

2. If the chilled dip is too thick, thin with additional yogurt. Transfer to a serving bowl and sprinkle with chopped cilantro. Serve chilled.

NOTE: Major Grey's chutney often contains large pieces of fruit, which should be finely chopped and then combined with some of the chutney syrup before using.

Faux Fondue

makes about 3 cups

MAKE-AHEAD: The dip can be prepared up to 1 day ahead.

Fondue works best for shorter parties; if it isn't stirred often, it can scorch on the bottom. This dip has many of the same flavors as fondue, but it can be kept warm for a longer period without any reservations.

1 tablespoon unsalted butter
1 small onion, chopped
1 tablespoon brandy
1 cup mayonnaise
2 cups (8 ounces) shredded
    Swiss cheese
½ cup freshly grated Parmesan

> **what to dip**
>
> Baguette slices • Broccoli and cauliflower florets, prepared for dipping (see page 85) • Carrot sticks • Celery sticks • Cherry tomatoes • Cucumber slices • Tiny new potatoes, cooked (see page 87) • Zucchini slices

1. Position a rack in the center of the oven and preheat the oven to 350°F.

2. Melt the butter in a small skillet over medium heat. Add the onion and cook, stirring often, until translucent, about 3 minutes. Remove from the heat and stir in the brandy.

3. Mix the mayonnaise with the Swiss and Parmesan cheeses in a medium bowl. Stir in the onion. Transfer to a heatproof 1-quart serving dish. (The dip can be prepared up to 1 day ahead, covered, and refrigerated. If it is chilled, increase the baking time accordingly.)

4. Bake until the dip is bubbly, about 30 minutes. Serve hot.

Moroccan Eggplant and Tomato Dip

makes about 3 cups

MAKE-AHEAD: The dip can be prepared up to 2 days ahead.

While preparing a Paula Wolfert recipe for chicken with tomato-eggplant "jam," I tasted the sauce on a piece of pita bread, and quickly realized its dip potential. The sauce soon appeared on my catering menu as a dip. The original recipe calls for frying the eggplant, but broiling is quicker and the results are lighter.

what to dip

Pita bread wedges •
Pita Toasts (page 179)

1 large eggplant
2 teaspoons salt, plus more as needed
6 tablespoons extra-virgin olive oil, or as needed
2 garlic cloves, minced
One 28-ounce can tomatoes in juice, drained and
    chopped
⅓ cup chopped fresh cilantro or parsley, plus more for
    garnish
2 tablespoons fresh lemon juice
1 teaspoon ground cumin
½ teaspoon sweet Hungarian paprika
Pinch of ground hot red (cayenne) pepper

1. Using a vegetable peeler, remove 1-inch lengthwise strips of peel all around the eggplant, leaving about an inch

or so between each one so that the eggplant looks striped when you are finished. Cut the eggplant into ½-inch rounds. Sprinkle both sides of the rounds with the 2 teaspoons salt, and place in a colander. Let stand in the sink for 1 to 2 hours to drain off the excess juice. Rinse quickly under cold water and pat dry with paper towels.

2. Position a broiler rack 6 inches from the heat source and preheat the broiler. Lightly oil the broiler rack. Brush both sides of the eggplant with about ¼ cup oil and place on the rack. Broil, turning once, until the eggplant is tender and golden brown, about 10 minutes. Transfer the eggplant to a food processor and puree.

3. Heat the remaining 2 tablespoons olive oil in a medium skillet over medium heat. Add the garlic and cook until fragrant, about 1 minute. Add the tomatoes and cook until the mixture has thickened, about 10 minutes. Stir in the eggplant puree, cilantro, lemon juice, cumin, paprika, and cayenne and bring to a boil. Reduce the heat to low and simmer, stirring often, until thick, about 5 minutes.

4. Season with salt, and let cool completely. Cover tightly and refrigerate until chilled, at least 2 hours, or up to 3 days.

5. Transfer to a serving bowl. Serve chilled or at room temperature, garnished with cilantro.

Herb-Garlic Vinaigrette

makes 1½ cups

MAKE-AHEAD: The vinaigrette can be prepared up to 3 days ahead.

When serving a heavy or complicated meal, a low-key nibble is in order. A bowl of crudités with an herbaceous vinaigrette can be very satisfying in its simplicity.

1 large egg
¼ cup red wine vinegar
1 tablespoon Dijon mustard
1 tablespoon finely chopped
  shallot
¾ cup extra-virgin olive oil
2 tablespoons chopped fresh
  herbs, such as thyme,
  rosemary, basil, parsley, and
  chives, in any combination
Salt and freshly ground black
  pepper to taste

what to dip

Broccoli and
cauliflower florets,
prepared for dipping
(see page 85) • Carrot
sticks • Celery sticks •
Cherry tomatoes •
Cucumber slices • Tiny
new potatoes, cooked
(see page 87) •
Zucchini slices

1. Place the egg in a small saucepan and add enough cold water to cover. Bring to a boil over high heat. Reduce the heat to medium and simmer for 2 minutes. Drain. Peel the egg—the white should be firm, the yolk barely set.

2. Combine the egg, vinegar, mustard, and shallot in a blender and pulse to combine. With the processor running, gradually add the oil, to make a thick vinaigrette. Add the herbs and pulse just to combine. Season with salt and pepper. Transfer to a small serving bowl, cover tightly and refrigerate to blend the flavors, at least 1 hour, or up to 3 days (if the vinaigrette separates, whirl in a food processor or blender to recombine).

3. Serve chilled.

Miso-Ginger Dip

makes 2 cups

MAKE-AHEAD: The dip can be prepared up to 2 days ahead.

M iso is essentially soybeans fermented in a grain base,
then ground into a paste. There are many different
kinds, all of which are very flavor-
ful. Brown rice miso is one of the
most versatile and easy to find, and
it lends its rich, salty flavor to this
smooth dip.

One 15-ounce can adzuki beans,
    drained and rinsed
3 tablespoons brown rice miso
    (available at natural food
    stores)
3 scallions, white and green
    parts, chopped
1 tablespoon shredded fresh
    ginger (use the large holes on
    a box grater)
2 tablespoons rice vinegar
2 garlic cloves, crushed through
    a press
⅓ cup water, or as needed
Hot red pepper sauce to taste

> **what to dip**
>
> Asparagus spears,
> prepared for dipping
> (see page 84) •
> Broccoli florets,
> prepared for dipping
> (see page 85) • Carrot
> sticks • Celery sticks •
> Cherry tomatoes •
> Cucumber slices •
> Green beans, prepared
> for dipping (see page
> 86) • Snow peas,
> prepared for dipping
> (see page 87) •
> Zucchini slices

1. Put the beans, miso, two-thirds of the scallions, the ginger, vinegar, and garlic in a food processor and pulse to combine. With the processor running, gradually add enough of the water to make a thick dip. Season with hot sauce. Transfer to a serving bowl. Cover tightly and refrigerate to blend the flavors, at least 1 hour, or up to 2 days.

2. Serve chilled or at room temperature, garnished with the remaining scallion.

Hot Mushroom and Swiss Dip

makes 3½ cups

MAKE-AHEAD: The dip can be prepared up to 1 day ahead.

It would be easy to make an entire meal out of this dip.

1 ounce dried porcini
   mushrooms, rinsed under
   cold water to remove grit
1 cup hot water
2 tablespoons unsalted butter
10 ounces assorted wild
   mushrooms, such as cremini
   and stemmed shiitake, finely
   chopped
¼ cup chopped shallots
2 teaspoons chopped fresh thyme or 1 teaspoon dried
   thyme
1 cup homemade or canned low-sodium chicken broth
1 cup milk
2 tablespoons all-purpose flour
2 cups (8 ounces) shredded Swiss cheese
⅓ cup freshly grated Parmesan
Salt and freshly ground black pepper to taste

> **what to dip**
>
> Broccoli and
> cauliflower florets,
> prepared for dipping
> (see page 85) • Carrot
> sticks • Celery sticks •
> Cherry tomatoes •
> Cucumber slices •
> Zucchini slices

1. Soak the dried mushrooms in the hot water in a small bowl until softened, about 20 minutes. Drain in a sieve

lined with moistened paper towels, reserving the soaking liquid. Coarsely chop the mushrooms.

2. Melt the butter in a large skillet over medium heat. Add the fresh mushrooms and cook, stirring often, until they give off their liquid, about 5 minutes. Add the chopped soaked mushrooms and their liquid and cook until the liquid evaporates and the mushrooms begin to brown, about 7 minutes. Stir in the shallots and thyme, and cook until the shallots are softened, about 1 minute.

3. Meanwhile, bring the broth and milk to a simmer in a small saucepan over medium heat, or use a microwave.

4. Sprinkle the mushrooms with the flour, mixing well. Reduce the heat to low and stir to cook the flour without browning, about 1 minute. Gradually whisk in the hot broth mixture. Bring to a simmer and cook until the dip is lightly thickened and no raw flour taste remains, about 5 minutes. Remove from the heat and stir in the Swiss and Parmesan cheeses until melted. Season with salt and pepper. (The dip can be prepared up to 1 day ahead, cooled, covered, and refrigerated. Reheat in a double boiler.)

5. Transfer to a heatproof serving dish. Serve hot.

Vidalia Onion Spread

makes about 1 cup

MAKE-AHEAD: The spread can be prepared up to 3 days ahead.

M y friend Kelly Volpe contributed this dip, which was created on a whim for a friend's birthday party. Be sure to use Vidalia, Maui, Texas Sweet, or other sweet onions, not the savory yellow Spanish variety. The spread is great on its own, but I like to serve blue cheese with it—the combination of sweet and salty is terrific.

what to spread

Baguette slices •
Crostini (page 180) •
Flatbread crisps •
Celery sticks

4 large sweet onions, quartered lengthwise
12 large garlic cloves, peeled
1 tablespoon extra-virgin olive oil
1 tablespoon honey
Salt and freshly ground black pepper to taste
2 tablespoons chopped fresh chives, plus more for garnish

1. Position a rack in the top third of the oven and preheat to the oven to 350°F. Lightly oil a 13 × 9-inch baking dish.

2. Toss the onions and garlic together in the baking dish. Whisk the oil and honey in a small bowl, drizzle over the

onions and garlic, and toss to coat. Season with salt and pepper.

3. Bake, stirring occasionally, until the onions are golden brown and tender, about 40 minutes. Let cool completely.

4. Puree the onions and garlic in a blender or food processor. Add the chives and pulse to mix. Transfer to a small bowl. Cover tightly and refrigerate until chilled, at least 2 hours, or up to 3 days.

5. Transfer to a serving bowl and sprinkle with chives. Serve chilled, with a small knife for spreading.

Pesto-Mascarpone Dip

makes about 1¾ cups

MAKE-AHEAD: The dip can be prepared up to 2 days ahead.

Mascarpone is a creamy cheese that cries out to be turned into a dip. Pesto gives a lift to its buttery flavor. To make the dip thin enough for fragile chips, add more sour cream or stir in some milk.

> **what to dip**
>
> Potato chips, store-bought or homemade (page 171 or 174) • Fresh baguette slices • Bruschetta (page 182) • Crostini (page 180) • Carrot sticks • Celery sticks • Cherry tomatoes • Cucumber slices • Zucchini slices

1 cup packed fresh basil leaves, plus a sprig for garnish
¼ cup freshly grated Parmesan
2 garlic cloves, crushed through a press
¼ cup extra-virgin olive oil
One 8½-ounce container mascarpone cheese, at room temperature
⅓ cup sour cream, or more as needed
Salt and freshly ground black pepper to taste

1.   Combine the basil, Parmesan, and garlic in a food processor and process until finely chopped. With the processor running, gradually add the oil, to make a puree. Add the mascarpone and sour cream and process, scraping down the bowl occasionally, until combined. If desired, add more

sour cream to get the desired thickness. Season with salt and pepper. Transfer to a small bowl, cover, and refrigerate until chilled, at least 2 hours, or up to 2 days.

2. Serve at room temperature, garnished with the sprig of basil.

Spicy Radish and Red Pepper Dip

makes about 3½ cups

MAKE-AHEAD: The dip can be prepared up to 1 day ahead.

When considering the radish, most cooks simply don't get past the salad bowl, but its peppery flavor is the beginning of a very tasty dip.

12 large radishes, scrubbed
One 12-ounce container
    whipped cream cheese
2 red bell peppers, roasted (see
    page 12), peeled, seeded, and
    chopped
½ cup sour cream
2 tablespoons chopped fresh
    chives, plus more for garnish
Salt and freshly ground black
    pepper to taste

what to dip

Potato chips, store-bought or homemade (pages 171 or 174) • Crostini (page 180) • Pita Toasts (page 179) • Flatbread crisps • Carrot sticks • Celery sticks • Cherry tomatoes • Cucumber slices • Zucchini slices

1. Using a food processor fitted with the shredding disk or the large holes of a box grater, shred the radishes. A handful at a time, squeeze out the excess moisture from the radishes.

2. With a rubber spatula, mash the cream cheese, radishes, roasted peppers, sour cream, and chives in a

medium bowl until combined. Season with salt and pepper. Cover and refrigerate until chilled, at least 2 hours, or overnight.

3. Transfer to a serving bowl and sprinkle with chopped chives. Serve chilled.

Raspberry–Poppy Seed Vinaigrette

makes 1½ cups

MAKE-AHEAD: The vinaigrette can be prepared up to 3 days ahead.

Sweet-and-sour dips spark the appetite, making this one a good choice for a not-too-filling appetizer before a big dinner. Raspberries give the dip a refreshingly fruity flavor and make it thick enough to cling to the most slippery crudités.

what to dip

Broccoli and cauliflower florets, prepared for dipping (see page 85) • Carrot sticks • Celery sticks • Cherry tomatoes • Cucumber slices • Zucchini slices

½ pint raspberries
¼ cup cider vinegar
¼ cup fresh orange juice
1 teaspoon sugar
1 teaspoon dry mustard
½ teaspoon salt
¼ teaspoon freshly ground
    black pepper
¾ cup vegetable oil
2 tablespoons poppy seeds

1.   Combine the raspberries, vinegar, orange juice, sugar, mustard, and salt in a food processor and pulse to combine. With the processor running, gradually pour in the oil to make a thick vinaigrette. Strain through a fine sieve

(remove the raspberry seeds) into a bowl. Stir in the poppy seeds. Cover and refrigerate until chilled, at least 1 hour, or up to 3 days.

2. Whisk well to recombine. Pour into a small serving bowl and serve chilled or at room temperature.

Sweet and Spicy
Red Pepper Dip

makes 2 cups

MAKE-AHEAD: The dip can be prepared up to 2 days ahead.

There are few dips more vibrantly colorful than this one. It's also another dip that is low in fat but high in flavor— serve it with crudités for a snack that will get high marks from your calorie-watching guests.

> **what to dip**
>
> Pita bread wedges • Baguette slices • Tortilla chips, store-bought or homemade (page 176) • Broccoli and cauliflower florets, prepared for dipping (see page 85) • Zucchini slices

2 tablespoons extra-virgin olive oil
1 large onion, chopped
1 jalapeño, seeded and minced
4 garlic cloves, minced
6 large red bell peppers, roasted (see page 12), peeled, and seeded
1 tablespoon plus 1 teaspoon red wine vinegar
1 tablespoon balsamic vinegar
1 tablespoon light brown sugar
1 teaspoon ground cumin
Salt to taste

1. Heat the oil in a large skillet over medium heat. Add the onion and jalapeño and cook uncovered, stirring often,

until the onion is browned, about 6 minutes. During the last minute, add the garlic. Let cool slightly.

2.   Combine the red peppers, onion and garlic, red wine vinegar, balsamic vinegar, brown sugar, and cumin in a food processor and process to a puree. Season with salt. Transfer to a medium bowl and let cool completely, then cover tightly and refrigerate until chilled, at least 1 hour, or up to 2 days.

3.   Transfer to a serving bowl and serve chilled.

Roasted Garlic Skordalia

makes about 4 cups

MAKE-AHEAD: The skordalia can be prepared up to 2 days ahead.

To call skordalia garlicky would be an understatement (the name derives from *skorda*, Greek for garlic). The classic recipe uses potatoes mashed with raw garlic (some versions use ground nuts or bread crumbs), and most Greeks make it so strong that it is spicy-hot. I like to use roasted garlic to tame the heat. One important tip: never use a food processor to puree potatoes, or you will end up with something that resembles a pot of glue. A potato ricer does the best job.

> ### what to dip
>
> Potato chips, store-bought or homemade (page 171 or 174) • Pita bread wedges • Pita Toasts (page 179) • Flatbread crisps • Carrot sticks • Celery sticks • Cherry tomatoes • Cucumber slices • Radishes • Zucchini slices

2 large baking (russet) potatoes (1¼ pounds), scrubbed
2 large heads garlic, roasted (see page 10)
¼ cup fresh lemon juice
¾ cup extra-virgin olive oil
Salt and freshly ground black pepper to taste

1. Place the potatoes in a large saucepan, cover with lightly salted water, and bring to a boil over high heat. Cook

until the potatoes are tender, about 35 minutes. Drain, reserving about 1 cup of the cooking liquid. Rinse the potatoes under cold water, and let cool until easy to handle.

2. Peel the potatoes. Press them through a potato ricer or rub through a wire sieve into a large bowl. Squeeze the cooled garlic from the skins into the bowl. Using a hand-held electric mixer or a whisk, beat in the lemon juice. Gradually beat in the oil, then beat in enough of the reserved potato liquid to make a smooth dip. Season with salt and pepper. Cover tightly and refrigerate until chilled, at least 2 hours, or up to 2 days.

3. Transfer the skordalia to a serving bowl, and serve at room temperature.

CLASSIC SKORDALIA   Substitute 4 garlic cloves, crushed through a press, for the roast garlic.

Sun-Dried Tomato Olivada

makes about 2 ½ cups

MAKE-AHEAD: The olivada can be prepared up to 2 days ahead.

Sun-dried tomatoes are one of those ingredients that make a cook wonder what one did without them in the old days (say, twenty years ago). They add a wallop of flavor to whatever they're in, and this spread is no exception. Adjust its thickness with a bit of extra oil or even water. Take care when seasoning, as some sun-dried tomatoes are quite salty.

> **what to spread**
>
> Baguette slices •
> Crostini (page 180) •
> Breadsticks, store-
> bought or homemade
> (page 184) • Flatbread
> crisps • Cherry
> tomatoes • Tiny
> new potatoes, cooked
> (see page 87) • Red
> bell pepper strips •
> Zucchini rounds

½ cup pitted and chopped black
    Mediterranean olives, such as
    Kalamata
½ cup drained and coarsely
    chopped oil-packed sun-dried
    tomatoes
1 large red bell pepper, roasted (see page 12), peeled,
    seeded, and cut into ¼-inch dice
2 tablespoons nonpareil capers, drained and rinsed
1 tablespoon chopped fresh basil
1 tablespoon chopped fresh oregano (or additional
    basil)
1 tablespoon red wine vinegar

1 tablespoon extra-virgin olive oil
1 garlic clove, crushed through a press
¼ teaspoon crushed hot red pepper
Salt to taste

1. Combine the olives, sun-dried tomatoes, roasted pepper, capers, basil, oregano, vinegar, oil, garlic, and hot pepper in a food processor and pulse until finely chopped but not pureed. Season with salt. Transfer to a medium bowl, cover, and refrigerate until chilled, at least 1 hour, or up to 3 days.

2. Transfer to a serving bowl. Serve chilled or at room temperature, with a small knife for spreading.

Tahini-Carrot Dip

makes 2 cups

MAKE-AHEAD: The dip can be prepared up to 2 days ahead.

Vegetable juice makes an interesting cooking ingredient. Bottled carrot juice, available at natural food stores, is perfect in this tahini dip, but do experiment with other freshly extracted juices from your local juice stand.

what to dip

Pita bread wedges • Broccoli and cauliflower florets, prepared for dipping (see page 85) • Carrot sticks • Celery sticks • Cherry tomatoes • Cucumber slices • Zucchini slices

1 cup tahini
¾ cup carrot juice, or as needed
¼ cup fresh lemon juice
1½ teaspoons chopped fresh
   rosemary
2 garlic cloves, crushed through
   a press
Salt and hot red pepper sauce,
   to taste
Chopped fresh parsley for garnish

1.   Combine the tahini, carrot juice, lemon juice, rosemary, and garlic in a blender. Blend until smooth, occasionally stopping the blender to scrape down the sides. Season with the salt and hot pepper sauce. Transfer to a serving bowl. Cover and refrigerate until chilled, at least 1 hour, or

up to 2 days. If the chilled dip is too thick, thin with additional carrot juice.

2. Sprinkle with parsley and serve chilled or at room temperature.

Tomato Romesco

makes about 1¼ cups

MAKE-AHEAD: The dip can be prepared up to 2 days ahead.

The Spanish use this deep pink sauce for shellfish, but there's no reason it shouldn't be used as a dip. If you wish, puree a roasted red pepper (see page 12) with the rest of the ingredients and use a bit more olive oil to thin the dip.

> **what to dip**
>
> Potato chips, store-bought or homemade (pages 171 or 174) • Baguette slices • Pita bread wedges • Pita Toasts (page 179) • Flatbread crisps • Carrot sticks • Celery sticks • Cherry tomatoes • Cucumber slices • Zucchini slices

⅓ cup sliced natural almonds
½ cup plus 2 tablespoons extra-virgin olive oil
1 small onion, finely chopped
2 large garlic cloves, minced
2 ripe plum tomatoes, peeled, seeded, and coarsely chopped (or use canned tomatoes)
1 tablespoon tomato paste
1 tablespoon fresh lemon juice
⅛ teaspoon ground hot red (cayenne) pepper
Salt to taste

1.   Heat a medium skillet over medium heat. Add the almonds and heat, stirring often, until toasted, about 2 minutes. Transfer to a plate and let cool.

2. Heat 2 tablespoons of the oil in the skillet over medium heat. Add the onion and cook until golden, about 4 minutes. Add the garlic and stir until fragrant, about 1 minute. Transfer to a blender or a food processor.

3. Add the tomatoes, tomato paste, lemon juice, and cayenne to the onions. With the processor running, gradually pour in the remaining ½ cup oil and process until thickened. Season with salt. Transfer to a bowl. Cover and refrigerate until chilled, at least 1 hour, or up to 2 days.

4. Transfer to a serving bowl. Serve chilled or at room temperature.

White Bean and
Roasted Garlic Dip

makes about 3 cups

MAKE-AHEAD: The dip can be prepared up to 3 days ahead.

Canned beans and garlic are always in my kitchen, so it's
no trouble at all to whip up a batch of this dip for
impromptu get-togethers. As for
what herb to use, I simply see what
needs to be trimmed back in the
garden.

> **what to dip**
>
> Bruschetta (page 182) •
> Crostini (page 180) •
> Flatbread crisps •
> Celery sticks • Cherry
> tomatoes • Fennel
> bulb, cut into sticks

Two 15½- to 19-ounce cans
    cannellini (white kidney
    beans)
1 large head garlic, roasted
    (see page 10)
1 tablespoon chopped fresh herbs, such as sage,
    rosemary, and/or thyme (preferably a combination
    of all three), or 1 teaspoon dried Italian seasoning
2 tablespoons fresh lemon juice
⅛ teaspoon crushed hot red pepper
⅓ cup extra-virgin olive oil, or as needed
Salt to taste

1.   Drain the beans, reserving the canning liquid if you
plan to refrigerate the dip overnight or longer. Rinse under
cold water and drain again.

2. Squeeze the roasted garlic flesh from the skin into a food processor. Add the beans, herbs, lemon juice, and red pepper. With the processor running, add enough of the oil to make a thick dip. Season with salt. Transfer to a bowl, cover tightly, and refrigerate until chilled, at least 1 hour, or up to 3 days.

3. If the chilled dip is too thick, thin with the reserved canning liquid as necessary. Transfer to a serving bowl and serve chilled or at room temperature.

Zucchini, Mint, and Garlic Dip

makes about 2 cups

MAKE-AHEAD: The dip can be prepared up to 2 days ahead.

Guilt-free dips don't come any more delicious than this one. It's based on *tzatziki,* the Greek cucumber dip. Shredded zucchini has more flavor than cucumber, and it gives the dip a pretty green color. For purists, I provide the cucumber version as a variation.

> **what to dip**
>
> Pita bread wedges •
> Pita Toasts (page 179) •
> Carrot sticks • Celery
> sticks • Cherry
> tomatoes • Cucumber
> slices

2 cups plain whole or low-fat
    yogurt (not nonfat)
2 medium zucchini (about
    14 ounces), trimmed
½ teaspoon salt, plus more to taste
4 teaspoons freshly chopped mint
1 garlic clove, crushed through a press
Freshly ground black pepper to taste

1.   Line a sieve with dampened paper towels and place over a medium bowl. Spoon the yogurt into the sieve and refrigerate for 1 hour, or until about ¾ cup of whey has drained from the yogurt.

2.   Meanwhile, shred the zucchini on the large holes of a box grater. Place in a bowl and toss with the ½ teaspoon

salt. Let stand for 1 hour. A handful at a time, squeeze the excess liquid from the zucchini.

3. Combine the drained yogurt, zucchini, mint, and garlic in a large bowl. Season with salt and pepper. Cover and refrigerate until chilled, at least 2 hours, or overnight.

4. Transfer to a serving bowl and serve chilled.

CLASSIC TZATZIKI Substitute 2 medium cucumbers, peeled, halved lengthwise, and seeds removed with the tip of a spoon, for the zucchini.

Tuscan Tomato and Basil Topping

makes 2 cups

MAKE-AHEAD: The topping is best served immediately.

Bruschetta with tomatoes is something you can find on most Italian restaurant menus year-round—but it shouldn't be. It should be made only with top-notch, flavorful summer tomatoes, not bland hothouse varieties. Vary the recipe by using the best-tasting tomatoes at the market: heirloom varieties, yellow tomatoes, or even chopped cherry tomatoes will all be wonderful.

> **what to spread**
>
> Bruschetta (page 182)

3 beefsteak tomatoes, halved, seeded, and cut into
   ½-inch cubes
¼ teaspoon salt
⅓ cup pitted and chopped black Mediterranean olives
2 tablespoons chopped fresh basil
2 tablespoons extra-virgin olive oil
1 garlic clove, crushed through a press, optional
⅛ teaspoon crushed hot red pepper

1.   Toss the tomato cubes with the salt in a colander. Let stand in a sink to drain off the excess juices, about 30 minutes.

2.   Mix the tomato cubes, olives, basil, oil, garlic, if using, and red pepper in a medium bowl. Serve immediately.

Rib-Sticking Meat and Seafood Dips

I think of these as my Super Bowl dips—the kind of rib-sticking fare that will satisfy the hungriest guy. Hearty and filling, some of these dips are so substantial they are actually spreads. (In fact, I look forward to having leftovers of the Ham and Swiss Cheese Spread or Italian Tuna and Caper Spread to use as sandwich fillings.) With one glance, you'll know whether or not to serve them with a knife.

For food safety reasons, it is important to keep these dips at their optimum serving temperature. Cold dips should be kept chilled, and hot dips warm, for no longer than two hours. See page 5 for suggestions on how to work within these restrictions.

Long Island Clam Dip

makes 2 cups

MAKE-AHEAD: The dip can be prepared up to 1 day ahead.

While old-fashioned clam dip may have its fans, canned clams are not an especially exciting item. So, when faced with a surplus of fresh steamed clams, I decided to accept the challenge of making a clam dip that I would serve to my friends. Be careful when seasoning the dip, because the clam cooking liquid can be salty. Use plump, meaty cherrystone clams; if only smaller littlenecks are available, increase the number of clams to twelve.

> **what to dip**
>
> Potato chips, store-bought or homemade (page 171 or 174) • Tortilla chips, store-bought or homemade (page 176) • Baguette slices • Crostini (page 180) • Flatbread crisps • Broccoli florets, prepared for dipping (see page 85) • Celery sticks • Cherry tomatoes

6 cherrystone clams, scrubbed, soaked in cold water to cover for 1 hour, and drained
1 small onion, sliced
1 cup water
2 garlic cloves, minced
1 tablespoon olive oil
One 8-ounce package cream cheese, at room temperature
¼ cup milk
2 scallions, white and green parts, finely chopped

2 tablespoons chopped fresh parsley
Salt and freshly ground black pepper to taste

1. Combine the clams, onion, and water in a large saucepan and bring to a boil over high heat. Cover tightly and cook until all of the clams open, about 7 minutes. Using tongs, transfer the clams to a platter to cool.

2. Strain the cooking liquid through a sieve lined with a moistened paper towel into a bowl. Rinse out the pot. Return 1 cup of the liquid to the pot (freeze the remaining liquid to use as a shellfish stock, if desired), and bring to a boil over high heat. Boil until the liquid has reduced to about 3 tablespoons, about 5 minutes. Let cool completely.

3. Cook the garlic in the oil in a small skillet over medium heat until soft and golden, about 2 minutes. Let cool completely.

4. Remove the clams from the shells, discarding the shells. Pulse the clams in a food processor fitted with the metal blade until coarsely chopped.

5. With a rubber spatula, mash the cream cheese, cooled clam juice, and milk in a medium bowl until smooth. Mix in the clams, garlic with its oil, scallions, and parsley. Season carefully with salt and pepper (the clams may be salty). Cover tightly with plastic wrap and refrigerate until chilled, at least 2 hours, or overnight.

6. Transfer to a serving bowl and serve chilled.

CLASSIC CLAM DIP   Drain one 7-ounce can minced clams, reserving the juice. Mash one 8-ounce package cream cheese, at room temperature, with the clam juice and 1 tablespoon grated onion. Mix in the clams. Season with salt and pepper. Chill and serve.

Hot Crab-Salsa Dip

makes about 4 cups

MAKE-AHEAD: The dip can be prepared up to 8 hours ahead, then baked just before serving.

B ecause I get so many requests whenever I serve this dip, I have gotten in the habit of printing out the recipe before the party. Be sure to use a very thick salsa. If it seems watery, drain in a wire sieve before using. Shrimp salsa dip sounds like a good idea too, but, unfortunately, shrimp can easily turn tough if heated for too long—stick to the crab version.

> **what to dip**
>
> Potato chips, store-bought or homemade (page 171 or 174) • Tortilla chips, store-bought or homemade (page 176) • Flatbread crisps • Broccoli florets, prepared for dipping (see page 85) • Celery sticks • Cherry tomatoes

One 8-ounce package cream
    cheese, at room temperature
1 cup mayonnaise
1 cup chunky tomato salsa
1 teaspoon Worcestershire
    sauce
1 pound fresh crabmeat, picked
    over to remove cartilage and flaked
Hot red pepper sauce
⅓ cup fresh bread crumbs, preferably from day-old
    French or Italian bread

1.   Position a rack in the center of the oven and preheat the oven to 350°F. Lightly butter a 1-quart round baking dish.

2. With a rubber spatula, mash the cream cheese, mayonnaise, salsa, and Worcestershire sauce in a medium bowl until combined. Stir in the crabmeat. Season with hot pepper sauce. Spread in the baking dish. (The dip can be prepared up to 8 hours ahead, covered tightly with plastic wrap, and refrigerated.)

3. Sprinkle the bread crumbs over the dip. Bake until the dip is bubbling, about 30 minutes or slightly longer if refrigerated. Serve hot.

Two-Salmon Dip

makes about 2 cups

MAKE-AHEAD: The dip can be prepared up to 1 day ahead.

Definitely a sophisticated dip, this is what I would serve for a special party where plenty of champagne is flowing. It also makes a great dip for a brunch.

Two 8-ounce containers
   whipped cream cheese
3 tablespoons milk
4 ounces thinly sliced smoked
   salmon, such as Nova
   (see Note), finely chopped
2 teaspoons finely chopped
   fresh chives, plus more for garnish
2 ounces salmon caviar
Freshly ground black pepper to taste

what to dip

Potato chips, store-bought or homemade (page 171 or 174) •
Matzo crackers •
Bagel chips •
Cucumber slices

1. Combine the whipped cream cheese and milk in a medium bowl and mash with a rubber spatula until smooth. Fold in the salmon and chives, then the caviar, being careful not to burst it. Season with pepper to taste. Cover and refrigerate until chilled, about 1 hour, or up to 1 day (if the chilled dip is too thick, thin with additional milk).

2. Transfer to a serving bowl and sprinkle with chives. Serve chilled.

> **NOTE:** I usually make this dip with thinly sliced delicatessen-style cold-smoked salmon. However, it is also delicious with flaked hot-smoked salmon fillet or steak.

Cajun Shrimp and Artichoke Dip

makes 3½ cups

MAKE-AHEAD: The dip can be prepared up to 1 day ahead.

If there was ever a crowd-pleasing dip, this is it. Spicy but not too wild, with chunks of shrimp and artichokes, it is the perfect dunk for everything from chips and crackers to crudités.

1 cup mayonnaise
1 cup sour cream
2 teaspoons Cajun Seasoning (see below) or salt-free store-bought seasoning
8 ounces cooked, peeled, and deveined shrimp, coarsely chopped
Two 6-ounce jars marinated artichoke hearts, drained and chopped
⅓ cup drained and coarsely chopped sun-dried tomatoes
3 scallions, white and green parts, finely chopped
Salt and freshly ground black pepper to taste

what to dip

Potato chips, store-bought or homemade (page 171 or 174) • Tortilla chips, store-bought or homemade (page 176) • Baguette slices • Crostini (page 180) • Flatbread crisps • Carrot sticks • Celery sticks • Cherry tomatoes • Cucumber slices • Mushroom caps • Zucchini slices

1. Mix the mayonnaise, sour cream, and Cajun Seasoning in a medium bowl. Add the shrimp, artichokes, sun-dried tomatoes, and scallions, mixing well. Season with salt and pepper. Cover and refrigerate to blend the flavors, at least 1 hour, or overnight.

2. Transfer to a serving bowl and serve chilled.

CAJUN SEASONING Mix 2 tablespoons sweet paprika, preferably Hungarian, 1 tablespoon dried basil, 1 tablespoon dried thyme, 1 teaspoon garlic powder, 1 teaspoon onion powder, ½ teaspoon freshly ground black pepper, and ¼ teaspoon ground hot red (cayenne) pepper. Makes about ⅓ cup. Use as a seasoning for dips, popcorn, salads, grilled foods, and in Cajun and Creole cooking.

Dilled Shrimp Spread

makes about 2¾ cups

MAKE-AHEAD: The spread can be prepared up to 1 day ahead.

For an elegant spread that comes together fast, spring for precooked shrimp at the market, and make this. For years, it was a staple at my catering company, piped onto cucumber slices or used as a filling for baked pastry hors d'oeuvres. Now I serve it as one of my favorite spreads.

what to spread

Baguette slices •
Crostini (page 180) •
Pita bread wedges •
Pita Toasts (page 179) •
Cucumber slices

12 ounces cooked shrimp, finely
   chopped
One 12-ounce container
   whipped cream cheese, at room temperature
2 tablespoons fresh lemon juice
1½ tablespoons chopped fresh dill, plus dill sprigs for
   garnish
½ teaspoon Worcestershire sauce
Hot red pepper sauce to taste

1.   With a rubber spatula, mash the shrimp, cream cheese, lemon juice, chopped dill, and Worcestershire sauce in a medium bowl until combined. Season with hot pepper sauce. Cover and refrigerate until chilled, at least 2 hours, or overnight.

2.   Just before serving, garnish with dill sprigs. Serve chilled.

Ham and Swiss Cheese Spread

makes about 2½ cups

MAKE-AHEAD: The spread can be prepared up to 2 days ahead.

Are the ingredients for this spread prosaic? Maybe. But some food combinations just can't be ignored, and ham and Swiss is at the top of the list. Try leftovers spread on toast and broiled until bubbling.

> **what to spread**
>
> Crisp rye crackers •
> Rye or pumpernickel
> bread slices, toasted •
> Flatbread crisps

One 3-ounce package cream cheese, at room temperature
½ cup mayonnaise
1 tablespoon Dijon mustard
1 tablespoon prepared horseradish
½ pound smoked ham, finely chopped in a food processor
2 cups (8 ounces) shredded sharp Swiss cheese
1 tablespoon shredded onion (use the large holes on a box grater)

1. With a rubber spatula, mash the cream cheese, mayonnaise, mustard, and horseradish in a medium bowl until smooth. Mix in the ham, Swiss cheese, and onion. Cover with plastic wrap and refrigerate until chilled, at least 2 hours, or overnight.

2. Transfer to a serving bowl and serve chilled.

Hell's Kitchen Taramasalata

makes 3 cups

MAKE-AHEAD: The dip can be prepared up to 2 days ahead.

Manhattan's Hell's Kitchen (sometimes called by its less colorful name, Clinton) has a collection of ethnic markets, but my favorite is International Grocers, where I buy most of my spices and Mediterranean ingredients. They are renowned for their taramasalata, a Greek dip made from salted carp roe, which is much lighter than anyone else's. The proprietors told me their secret: seltzer. (They also use a bit of almond flour, but I find it isn't an essential ingredient.) The hardest part is locating the tarama, which can be found at Mediterranean grocers, sold either in bulk from the delicatessen refrigerator or in jars.

> **what to dip**
>
> Pita bread wedges •
> Pita Toasts (page 179) •
> Potato chips, store-
> bought or homemade
> (page 171 or 174)

1 large (9-ounce) baking (russet) potato, peeled and
   cut into 1-inch chunks
½ cup fresh bread crumbs, made from firm country-
   style bread
½ cup (5 ounces) tarama (salted carp roe, available at
   Mediterranean grocers)
¾ cup olive oil (not extra-virgin)
2 tablespoons fresh lemon juice

1 tablespoon grated onion (use the large holes on a box grater)
2 tablespoons seltzer, or as needed
Chopped fresh parsley for garnish

1. Bring the potato and enough lightly salted water to cover to a boil in a medium saucepan over high heat. Reduce the heat to medium and cook until the potato is tender, about 20 minutes. Drain well, and transfer to a medium bowl.

2. Soak the bread crumbs in cold water to cover for 1 minute. Drain in a sieve and press out the water. Add to the potato.

3. Using a hand-held electric mixer on medium speed, beat the potatoes and soaked crumbs to combine. Add the tarama, then beating on low speed, add the oil drop by drop (it should take at least 1 minute to add the oil), to make a thick sauce. Add the lemon juice and onion, then add enough of the seltzer to make a light, fluffy dip. Cover and refrigerate until chilled, at least 1 hour, or up to 2 days.

4. Transfer to a serving bowl. Sprinkle with parsley and serve chilled.

Smoked Trout Brandade

makes about 2 cups

MAKE-AHEAD: The spread can be prepared up to 2 days ahead.

Brandade, a puree of salt cod and potatoes, is a French classic. Frankly, though, in America, salt cod isn't a very popular ingredient (at least not with my friends). My version uses smoked trout, an excellent substitute. Don't be tempted to experiment with other smoked fish: I have, and they are usually too rich.

what to dip

Potato chips, store-bought or homemade (page 171 or 174) • Baked Potato Skins (page 178) • Baguette slices • Crostini (page 180) • Cucumber slices

3 medium (7-ounce) baking (russet) potatoes, scrubbed
2 cups (10 ounces) flaked boneless smoked trout
1 garlic clove, crushed through a press
¼ cup heavy cream
¼ cup extra-virgin olive oil
Freshly ground black pepper to taste
Chopped fresh chives or parsley for garnish

1. Position a rack in the center of the oven and preheat the oven to 400°F.

2. Place the potatoes directly on the oven rack. Bake until tender, about 1 hour. Let cool until easy to handle.

3. Halve the potatoes and scoop the flesh out of the skins into a food processor (reserve the potato skins for dipping, if you like). Add the smoked fish and garlic. With the processor running, add the heavy cream and oil, blending until smooth. Season with pepper and transfer to a serving bowl. Cover tightly and refrigerate until chilled, at least 2 hours, or up to 2 days.

4. Transfer to a serving bowl. Serve chilled.

Italian Tuna and Caper Spread

makes about 1¾ cups

MAKE-AHEAD: The spread can be prepared up to 2 days ahead.

This is another spread that I can usually make without a trip to the grocery store for special ingredients, so it gets a workout. My pantry is always stocked with canned tuna, capers, and anchovy paste. Make this with flavorful imported Italian tuna packed in olive oil, if you can, although you'll find that American brands in vegetable oil or even water will work.

> **what to spread**
>
> Baguette slices •
> Crostini (page 180) •
> Flatbread crisps •
> Cherry tomatoes •
> Cucumber slices

Two 7-ounce cans tuna in olive oil, drained
½ cup mayonnaise
2 tablespoons fresh lemon juice
1 teaspoon anchovy paste
1 garlic clove, crushed through a press
3 tablespoons nonpareil capers, drained and rinsed
2 tablespoons chopped fresh parsley, plus more for garnish
Salt and freshly ground black pepper to taste

1. Combine the tuna, mayonnaise, lemon juice, and anchovy paste in a food processor and pulse until smooth.

Add the capers and parsley and pulse until combined. Season with salt and pepper. Transfer to a medium bowl and cover with plastic wrap. Refrigerate until chilled, at least 2 hours, or up to 2 days.

2.   Transfer to a serving bowl. Garnish with chopped parsley and serve chilled.

Hot Beef and Pinto Bean Chili Dip

makes 6 cups

MAKE-AHEAD: The dip can be prepared up to 2 days ahead.

Your Super Bowl party will be even more super with this meaty dip. It's equally good made with ground pork or the meat loaf combination of ground beef, pork, and veal.

1 tablespoon olive oil

1 medium onion, chopped

1 medium green bell pepper, cored seeded, and chopped

2 garlic cloves, chopped

1 jalapeño, seeded and minced

1½ pounds ground sirloin or round

2 tablespoons chili powder

2 teaspoons ground cumin

1 teaspoon dried oregano

One 14½-ounce can diced tomatoes in juice

One 8-ounce can tomato sauce

½ cup lager beer

1 teaspoon salt

½ teaspoon ground black pepper

One 15½- to 19-ounce can pinto beans, drained and rinsed

1 cup sour cream for garnish

1 cup (4 ounces) shredded extra-sharp Cheddar for garnish

> **what to dip**
>
> Tortilla Chips, store-bought or homemade (page 176) • Corn chips

1. Heat the oil in a large saucepan over medium heat. Add the onion, bell pepper, garlic, and jalapeño and cook, stirring often, until the onion softens, about 6 minutes. Add the beef and cook, stirring and breaking up the meat with the side of a spoon, until the meat loses its pink color, about 10 minutes. Drain off the fat.

2. Add the chili powder, cumin, and oregano and stir for 30 seconds. Stir in the tomatoes with their juice, the tomato sauce, beer, salt, and pepper. Bring to a simmer. Reduce the heat to medium-low and cook until thickened, about 45 minutes. During the last 10 minutes, add the beans. Remove from the heat and let stand for 5 minutes, then skim the fat that has risen to the surface. (The dip can be prepared up to 2 days ahead. Reheat gently over medium-low heat.)

3. Transfer to a heatproof serving bowl. Spoon the sour cream in the center, sprinkle the cheese around the sour cream, and serve hot.

Hot Beefed-Up Cheese Dip

makes 6 cups

MAKE-AHEAD: The dip can be prepared up to 1 day ahead.

Chile con queso made with "real" cheese is in a class by itself, but let's face it—most of the chile con queso in this country is prepared with good old pasteurized cheese product, aka Velveeta. There are those who argue that chile con queso is really an American invention, like chop suey, and that it is therefore OK to use Velveeta instead of cheese. (In Mexico, the hot cheese dip is usually called *queso fundido.*) In any event, the main advantage to using the pasteurized cheese product is that it melts smoothly and can be kept warm without separating for long periods. With the addition of ground beef, perhaps this should be called "chili con queso."

> ## what to dip
>
> Tortilla chips,
> store-bought or
> homemade (page 176) •
> Corn chips

1 tablespoon vegetable oil
1 pound ground round
One 8-ounce jar thick and chunky salsa
1½ pounds pasteurized prepared cheese product, such
    as Velveeta, cubed

1. Heat the oil in a medium skillet over medium heat. Add the ground round and cook, stirring and breaking up the meat with the side of a spoon, until cooked through, about 10 minutes. Pour off the fat from the skillet.

2. Add the salsa and bring to a simmer. Gradually stir in the cheese product until melted. (The dip can be prepared up to 1 day ahead, cooled, covered, and refrigerated. Reheat in a large stainless steel bowl set over a saucepan of boiling water.)

3. Transfer to a heatproof serving bowl and serve hot.

Bacon and Cheddar Dip

makes 3 cups

MAKE-AHEAD: The dip can be prepared up to 2 days ahead.

This dip may be sinfully rich, but it is worth any extra amount of time spent at the gym. I wonder what it would taste like with turkey bacon, reduced-fat cheese, reduced-fat mayonnaise, and nonfat sour cream? I didn't have the heart to make it that way. . . .

6 bacon slices
1 cup (4 ounces) shredded
   extra-sharp Cheddar
1 cup mayonnaise
1 cup sour cream
3 scallions, white and green
   parts, finely chopped
Hot red pepper sauce to taste

> **what to dip**
>
> Potato chips, store-bought or homemade (page 171 or 174) • Tortilla chips, store-bought or homemade (page 176) • Baguette slices • Crostini (page 180) • Flatbread crisps • Broccoli florets, prepared for dipping (see page 85) • Carrot sticks • Celery sticks • Cherry tomatoes • Zucchini slices

1. Cook the bacon in a large skillet over medium heat until browned and crisp, about 6 minutes (starting the bacon in a cold skillet reduces shrinkage and splattering). Transfer to paper towels to drain and cool.

2. Chop the bacon. Wrap and refrigerate 2 tablespoons for the garnish.

3. Stir the cheese, mayonnaise, sour cream, the remaining bacon, and two-thirds of the scallions together in a bowl. Season with hot pepper sauce. Cover and refrigerate until chilled, at least 2 hours, or up to 2 days.

4. Transfer to a serving bowl and top with the reserved bacon and the remaining scallions. Serve chilled.

New Mexican Pork and Green Chile Dip

makes 4 cups

MAKE-AHEAD: The dip can be prepared up to 1 day ahead.

In the roadside diners of New Mexico, the menu often features green chile, made with plenty of the local green chiles. (It's so popular, it's even on breakfast menus!) Served with tortilla chips, it makes a sinus-clearing dip.

> **what to dip**
>
> Tortilla chips,
> store-bought or
> homemade (page 176) •
> Corn chips

1 tablespoon olive oil
1 pound ground pork
Tomatillo-Cilantro Salsa
    (page 58)
3 mild chiles, such as Anaheim, New Mexico, or
    poblano, roasted (see page 8), peeled, seeded, and
    chopped
Salt to taste
1 cup (4 ounces) shredded Monterey Jack for garnish

1. Heat the oil in a large skillet over medium heat. Add the pork and cook, stirring and breaking up the pork with the side of a spoon, until it loses its pink color, about 10 minutes. Drain off the fat.

2. Add the salsa and chiles and bring to a boil. Reduce the heat to low and simmer uncovered, stirring often, until

thickened, about 10 minutes. (The dip can be prepared up to 1 day ahead, cooled, covered, and refrigerated. Reheat gently over medium-low heat.)

3. Transfer to a heatproof serving dish. Top with the cheese and serve hot.

Italian Mama Tomato and Pepperoni Dunk

makes 4½ cups

MAKE-AHEAD: The dip can be prepared up to 2 days ahead.

To inaugerate the first viewing of the complete DVD version of *The Godfather*, a new dip was in order. Mama Corleone would have been proud to serve this spicy tomato sauce as a dip for crusty bread.

> **what to dip**
>
> Baguette slices •
> Crostini (page 180) •
> Store-bought soft breadsticks

2 tablespoons extra-virgin olive oil
1 medium onion, chopped
8 ounces mushrooms, chopped
6 ounces thinly sliced pepperoni, chopped
2 garlic cloves, minced
½ cup hearty red wine, such as Shiraz
One 28-ounce can crushed tomatoes in thick puree
2 teaspoons dried oregano
¼ cup chopped fresh basil

1.   Heat the oil in a large saucepan over medium heat. Add the onion and cook, stirring often, until translucent, about 3 minutes. Add the mushrooms and cook, stirring often, until they give off their juices and they evaporate, about 6 minutes. Stir in the pepperoni and garlic and cook until the garlic is fragrant, about 1 minute.

2. Add the red wine and bring to a boil. Stir in the crushed tomatoes and oregano and bring back to a boil. Reduce the heat to low and simmer until thickened, about 45 minutes.

3. Stir in the basil and simmer for 5 minutes. (The dip can be prepared up to 2 days ahead, cooled, covered, and refrigerated. Reheat over medium heat.)

4. Transfer to a heatproof serving dish and serve hot.

Antipasti Salsa

makes about 5 cups

MAKE-AHEAD: The salsa can be prepared up to 2 days ahead.

Packed with a load of Italian goodies, this chunky mixture resembles a Mexican salsa more than anything else. It's the perfect opener to a Mediterranean-inspired menu.

1½ tablespoons red wine
vinegar
1 garlic clove, crushed through
a press
¼ cup extra-virgin olive oil
One 10-ounce package frozen artichoke hearts,
thawed
1 large red bell pepper, roasted (see page 12), seeded,
peeled, and chopped
2 medium celery ribs with leaves, finely chopped
2 tablespoons chopped fresh basil
⅛ teaspoon crushed hot red pepper
½ cup chopped Italian salami (2 ounces)
½ cup (2 ounces) chopped provolone
¼ cup pine nuts, toasted (see Note)
Salt to taste

> **what to dip**
>
> Baguette slices •
> Crostini (page 180) •
> Focaccia, cut into
> bite-sized pieces

1. Combine the vinegar and garlic in a medium bowl. Gradually whisk in the oil. Add the artichoke hearts,

roasted red pepper, celery, basil, and crushed red pepper and mix well. Cover and refrigerate until chilled, at least 1 hour, or up to 2 days.

2. Stir in the salami, cheese, and pine nuts. Season with salt. Transfer to a serving bowl and serve chilled, with a small spoon for scooping.

NOTE: To toast pine nuts, heat a small skillet over medium heat. Add the pine nuts and cook, stirring often, until lightly toasted, about 3 minutes. Transfer to a plate and cool completely.

Chicken Liver and Apple Spread

makes about 2½ cups

MAKE-AHEAD: The spread can be prepared up to 2 days ahead.

Get all those images of delicatessen chopped chicken liver out of your head. Apples and Calvados (French apple brandy, but you can use applejack, other brandy, or bourbon, if you wish) give this spread an extra dose of sophistication. It's terrific served on crackers and other crunchy usual suspects, but try it on tart apple slices too.

what to spread

Flatbread crisps •
Matzo crackers •
Bagel crisps •
Rye crackers

8 tablespoons (1 stick) unsalted butter, at room
    temperature
1 Granny Smith apple, peeled, cored, and cut into
    ½-inch dice
¼ cup chopped shallots
1 pound chicken livers, trimmed
¼ cup Calvados, applejack, brandy, or bourbon
1 teaspoon chopped fresh thyme or ½ teaspoon dried
    thyme
½ teaspoon salt
¼ teaspoon freshly ground black pepper
¼ cup heavy cream

1. Melt 1 tablespoon of the butter in a medium skillet over medium heat. Add the apple and cook, stirring often, until softened, about 5 minutes. Add the shallots and cook until the shallots and apple are tender, about 2 minutes. Transfer to a bowl and wipe out the skillet.

2. Melt 1 tablespoon of the butter in the skillet over medium-high heat. Add half of the chicken livers and cook, stirring occasionally, just until they are firm and slightly pink in the center when cut with a sharp knife, about 6 minutes. Transfer to a bowl. Repeat with another tablespoon of butter and the remaining livers. Let cool completely.

3. Heat the Calvados in a small saucepan over medium heat until warm. Carefully ignite the Calvados with a long match, averting your face. Let flame for about 20 seconds, then extinguish the flame by covering the pan tightly. Remove from the heat.

4. Combine the chicken livers, apple and shallots, thyme, salt, and pepper in a food processor; pulse to blend. With the processor running, add the remaining 5 tablespoons butter and the heavy cream. Transfer to a serving bowl or crock, cover, and refrigerate until chilled, at least 4 hours, or overnight.

5. Serve chilled, with a small knife for spreading.

Chips and Other Dippers

A dip without a dipper is a lonely thing. I have been known to say, "This dip is so great, I could eat the whole bowl with a spoon," but I really didn't mean it.

The most common way to get chips is to buy a bag and open it. Homemade chips, like from-scratch dips, are fun to make and definitely a step above what you can buy. That's not to say that there's anything wrong with store-bought chips! Personally, I've never met a potato chip I didn't like, from a bag or from my own kettle. Special occasions deserve special chips.

Beware of serving salted chips with salty dips—the salt level can become overwhelming. These include dips made with instant soup mixes, smoked fish, caviar, or salted roe (such as the Greek *tarama* in taramasalata). One of the benefits of making your own chips is that you control the amount of salt sprinkled on top. For store-bought chips, consider the unsalted or lightly salted versions. Those sturdy, ridged potato chips for dipping really are better, because the standard chip can be too thin for sturdy dips.

Tortilla chips are the perfect size and strength for dipping, and they hold up to the thickest, gloppiest dunk. They now come in an assortment of flavors and colors—just be careful to make a good match. Bean tortilla chips with bean dip is overkill.

There is a whole world of dippers beyond the beloved chip. The dipper should be compatible with the dip. For example, Mediterranean-inspired dips are usually best with pita bread or baguette slices, fresh or toasted. Dips with Asian flavors love being served with Vietnamese shrimp crackers. Pappadums are almost a must for curried dips. Tortilla chips with Provençal tapenade? I don't think so. . . .

A trip to an ethnic grocer will reveal an amazing assortment of creative dippers in a variety of colors and shapes that are guaranteed to jazz up the chip bowl. Most of them are deep-fried for serving (see Tips for Deep-Frying, page 169). Here are a few suggestions, culled from just one trip to my local ethnic supermarket.

COLORED TAPIOCA CRACKERS/*KRUPUK WARNA WARNI* (INDONESIAN) Red, green, gold, and orange, these round crackers made from tapioca flour sport an unusual squiggle pattern. Deep-fry at 360°F in batches, without crowding, turning once, until puffed and crisp, about 3 minutes. Drain on layers of crumpled paper towels, separating each layer with more towels.

FAR FAR (INDIAN) These look like colored squares of flat pasta, but they are made from potato starch, rice flour, and flour. Deep-fry at 360°F in batches, without crowding, until puffed, about 20 seconds. Drain on layers of crumpled paper towels, separating each layer with more towels.

GARLIC-FLAVORED CRACKERS/*KRUPUK BAWANG* (INDO-NESIAN) These are small (¾-inch-diameter) round tapioca crackers. Fry as for Far Far.

ONION RINGS (INDIAN) Potato, rye, and wheat flours combine to make these bright orange onion-flavored rings. Save them for thin dips. Fry as for Far Far.

PAPAD AND PAPPADUM (INDIAN) Large, spiced round wafers made from lentil flour. Papad have less baking soda than paddadum and don't puff as much. You may also see small (1-inch-diameter) wafers that make delicious dippers. Well-stocked Indian markets may have a variety of flavors, including cumin, chile, garlic, and black pepper. Heat about 1½ inches of vegetable oil in a deep skillet to 360°F. To deep-fry individual wafers, add one at a time to the oil, submerging with tongs, until puffed, about 5 seconds.

Transfer with the tongs to crumpled paper towels to drain, blotting each wafer gently with towels to remove excess oil. The wafers should be served whole; allow guests to break off pieces as they wish. To deep-fry small wafers, add about a dozen at a time to the hot oil and fry until puffed. Use a wire skimmer to transfer to crumpled paper towels.

SHRIMP AND CRAB CRACKERS (CHINESE) Asian markets carry these fried and sold in cellophane bags, just like potato chips, or boxed and ready to deep-fry yourself. Fry the thin, almost transparent uncooked chips as for Far Far.

Tips for Deep-Frying

• Deep-fried foods should really "swim" in the hot oil. Be generous with the amount of fat you add to the pot—it should come at least 3 inches up the sides.

• Use a deep-frying thermometer to judge the temperature of the oil. Adding the food to the oil will drop the temperature, so deep-fry the food at high heat to keep the temperature as steady as possible. Allow the oil to return to the proper cooking temperature before frying subsequent batches.

• Never crowd the ingredients in the oil. It's a sure way to get soggy fried food.

• A large wire-mesh skimmer, available at Asian markets, works best for removing deep-fried foods from hot oil.

- Most deep-fried food should be drained on a thick layer of crumpled paper towels. As soon as the oil has been re-bottled (see below), transfer the food to a large open receptacle, such as a baking pan. Store uncovered at room temperature. If stored in paper towels for too long, the food stays hot and creates steam that can render the food soggy.

- Cool and strain the deep-frying oil. Store, refrigerated, for up to 2 months. I don't recommend using all of the oil the next time you deep-fry, but do add about 1 tablespoon of old oil to every cup of new oil. This will improve both the flavor and the browning ability of the new oil. (Frying in "used" oil is one reason home-cooked French fries are different from those you get at a burger joint.)

Homemade Potato Chips

makes 4 to 6 servings

MAKE-AHEAD: The chips can be prepared up to 6 hours ahead.

For extra-special occasions, take the time to fry up a batch of potato chips. (For a rainbow of chips, make the carrot, parsnip, and beet variations too.) In addition to the ones on pages 172–173, here are a couple more tips for chips: First, be sure to use starchy brown-skinned potatoes, the bigger and older the better. Second, do not try to cut the chips by hand—a mandoline or a similar slicer is imperative. And, finally, don't salt the chips until just before serving, as the salt could wilt them.

1½ pounds large baking (russet) potatoes, peeled
Vegetable oil for deep-frying
Salt to taste

1.   Using a mandoline or plastic vegetable slicer, cut the potatoes into paper-thin rounds, less than $\frac{1}{16}$ inch thick. As they are cut, place in a bowl of cold water. Let stand while you heat the oil.

2.   Place a wire cake rack on a jelly-roll pan. Line a roasting pan with crumpled paper towels. Pour enough oil into a deep Dutch oven to come about 3 inches up the sides. Heat

the oil over high heat until a deep-frying thermometer reads 350°F.

3. Drain the potatoes well. Line a work surface with paper towels and spread one layer of potatoes on it. Cover with paper towels and continue layering, separating each layer of potatoes with more paper towels. Pat the potatoes completely dry.

4. In batches, without crowding, deep-fry the potatoes, stirring often with a wire-mesh skimmer to separate the chips, until they are golden brown, 2 to 3 minutes. Using the skimmer, transfer the chips to the wire rack to drain briefly, then move them to the crumpled paper towels to remove excess oil. Separate each layer of fried chips with more paper towels.

5. As soon as all the chips have been fried and drained, serve or transfer to a large roasting pan to store. The potato chips will crisp as they cool. Store uncovered, and serve within 6 hours.

6. Just before serving, sprinkle with salt.

CARROT OR PARSNIP CHIPS   Using a mandoline or plastic vegetable slicer, cut carrots or parsnips lengthwise into strips less than $1/16$ inch thick. Soak, drain, dry, and deep-fry as for potato chips.

BEET CHIPS Rub your hands lightly with vegetable oil to keep the juice from staining your skin. Peel the beets. Using the mandoline or plastic vegetable slicer, cut crosswise into rounds less than $\frac{1}{16}$ inch thick. Soak, drain, dry, and deep-fry as for potato chips. (If deep-frying a variety of chips, fry the beets last, as their juice can color the oil.)

Baked Potato Chips

makes 4 to 6 servings

MAKE-AHEAD: The chips can be prepared up to 6 hours ahead.

Food writer David Bonom taught me how to make baked potato chips, which are a fine alternative to deep-frying. The only drawback is that you can fit only two sheets of chips in the oven at one time, and that doesn't make for very quick cooking. Get yourself into an assembly line frame of mind, and bake them while you are doing other kitchen chores—you'll be surprised how quickly the job goes. For best results, use kitchen parchment paper and large heavy-gauge baking sheets measuring about 17 by 12 inches (called half-sheet pans, these are available at kitchenware stores).

Vegetable oil spray
1½ pounds large baking (russet) potatoes
Salt to taste

1.   Position the racks in the center and top third of the oven and preheat the oven to 375°F. Line two large baking sheets with parchment paper. Spray the paper with oil.

2.   Peel the potatoes placing them in a bowl with cold water to cover. Remove 1 potato from the water and pat dry. Using a mandoline or plastic vegetable slicer, cut the

potato into paper-thin rounds, less than $\frac{1}{16}$ inch thick, cutting only enough slices at a time to spread in single layers on the baking sheets. Arrange the slices on the sheets and spray slices with oil.

3. Bake until the chips are evenly golden brown, about 20 minutes (the chips on the center rack may take a few extra minutes). Slide the sheets of parchment onto a work surface and cool the chips on the parchment. Repeat with the remaining potatoes. Store uncovered, or use within 6 hours.

4. Just before serving, sprinkle with salt.

Fried Tortilla Chips

makes 4 to 6 servings

MAKE-AHEAD: The chips can be prepared up to 8 hours ahead.

Freshly fried tortilla chips turn a bowl of salsa into a fiesta. Look for high-quality corn tortillas at Latino markets—they will be fresher than the typical supermarket variety and contain fewer preservatives. The crispest chips are made from slightly stale tortillas, but fresh ones can be baked to dry them out before frying.

12 corn tortillas, cut into sixths
Vegetable oil for deep-frying
Salt to taste

1. Position the racks in the center and top third of the oven and preheat the oven to 300°F.

2. Spread the tortilla wedges on two baking sheets. Bake, switching the positions of the sheets from top to bottom halfway through baking, until the tortillas are slightly dried, about 10 minutes. Remove from the oven and let cool completely. (You can skip this procedure if your tortillas are stale.)

3. Line a baking sheet with crumpled paper towels and set aside. Pour enough oil into a deep Dutch oven to come about 3 inches up the sides. Heat over high heat until a deep-frying thermometer reads 365°F. In batches, without crowding, deep-fry the tortillas until golden brown, about 1 minute. Using a wire-mesh skimmer, transfer to paper towels to drain and cool, separating each layer of chips with more paper towels. As soon as all of the chips are fried and drained, transfer to a large roasting pan to store. (The chips can be prepared up to 8 hours ahead and stored uncovered at room temperature.)

4. Just before serving, sprinkle with salt.

BAKED TORTILLA CHIPS   Spread the dried (or stale) tortilla wedges in single layers on two baking sheets and spray with vegetable oil. Turn and spray again. Bake in a preheated 375°F oven until the tortillas are crisp, 10 to 15 minutes. Halfway through baking, stir the tortillas and switch the positions of the racks from top to bottom.

Baked Potato Skins

makes 4 servings

MAKE-AHEAD: The potato skins can be prepared up to 8 hours ahead, but they should be baked just before serving.

You'll have leftover potato skins after baking the potatoes for Smoked Trout Brandade (page 148). It's a shame to throw them out, and it's easy to turn them into scoopers for the dip. Baked potato skins are so tasty that you may find yourself baking potatoes just for the skins.

3 medium (7-ounce) baking (russet) potatoes, baked as
    directed on page 148
Vegetable oil or olive oil spray
Salt and freshly ground black pepper to taste

1.   Split the baked potatoes, scoop out the flesh, and use as desired. Cut the potato skins crosswise into thirds. (The potato skins can be prepared to this point up to 8 hours ahead, covered, and refrigerated.)

2.   Position a rack in the top third of the oven and preheat the oven to 400°F. Spray a baking sheet with vegetable oil.

3.   Arrange the potato skins skin side down on the baking sheet and spray with oil.

4.   Bake until the skins are crisp, about 20 minutes. Season with salt and pepper. Serve warm.

Pita Toasts

makes 6 to 8 servings

MAKE-AHEAD: The toasts can be prepared up to 8 hours ahead.

Crispy pita toasts can be prepared plain or seasoned with an herb to complement the dip you are serving. One of my favorites is zahtar, an herb blend that goes perfectly with many of the Middle Eastern–inspired dips, such as baba ganoush or hummus bi tahini. Zahtar is a mixture of ground sumac (from a dried tart berry), thyme, and sesame seeds. (There is also a Moroccan wild herb called za'tar, but it is different.) You'll find it at Mediterranean grocers—or you can just use a blend of sesame and oregano.

> 4 pita breads, split and each half cut into sixths
> ¼ cup extra-virgin olive oil, or as needed
> 2 teaspoons zahtar seasoning or 1 teaspoon each
>   sesame seeds and dried oregano, optional

1. Position the racks in the center and top third of the oven and preheat the oven to 350°F.

2. Spread the pita wedges cut sides up on the baking sheets and brush with the oil. Sprinkle with the zahtar, if using. Bake until crisp and golden, switching the position of the sheets from top to bottom halfway through baking, 10 to 15 minutes. Let cool completely. (The toasts can be prepared up to 8 hours ahead and stored uncovered at room temperature.)

Crostini

makes 6 to 8 servings

MAKE-AHEAD: The crostini can be prepared up to 8 hours ahead.

Crunchy crostini (meaning "crusts" in Italian) are baguette slices anointed with olive oil and baked, and are the perfect foil for many dips and spreads. If you wish, use the flavored breads, such as olive or herb, that can be found at many bakeries. But look for a bakery that makes loaves with a firm crumb without a lot of air pockets.

**1 baguette or baguette-shaped Italian bread, sliced
¼ inch thick (for larger slices, cut on the diagonal)
¼ cup extra-virgin olive oil**

1.   Position the racks in the center and top third of the oven and preheat the oven to 400°F.

2.   Spread the bread on two baking sheets. Brush the bread with the oil. Bake, switching the position of the sheets from top to bottom halfway through baking, until the toasts are golden brown, about 10 minutes. Transfer to wire racks to cool. (The toasts can be prepared up to 8 hours ahead and stored in a paper bag. Do not store in a plastic bag, which would soften the toasts.)

GARLIC CROSTINI   Heat 2 garlic cloves, crushed under a heavy knife and peeled, in the oil in a small saucepan over medium-low heat just until bubbles form around the garlic. Remove from the heat and let stand for 30 minutes. Use the garlic oil to brush the bread.

HERBED CROSTINI   Brush the bread with the plain or garlic olive oil. Sprinkle with about 2 tablespoons dried basil, oregano, or rosemary, or a combination.

Bruschetta

MAKE-AHEAD: The bruschetta can be prepared up to 2 hours ahead.

Look at just about any Italian restaurant menu in this country, and you'll see some kind of bruschetta. Bruschetta should not be just any old toast, but a grilled slice of chewy, crusty bread (although it is sometimes broiled, even in Italy). The word comes from the Italian *bruciare*, which means to burn or toast. In Tuscany and Umbria, if you ask for bruschetta, they will look puzzled, for there they call it *fett'unta*, for *fetta unta*, or anointed bread. I used to serve bruschetta only in the summer, when I did most of my grilling. With the introduction of gas grills, it can be served year-round, as long as the dip itself reflects the season. There are many other toppings beyond tomato—try the White Bean and Roasted Garlic Dip on page 128.

> Twelve (¼- to ½-inch-thick) slices cut from a large
>   round loaf of crusty country-style bread
> 2 to 3 garlic cloves, peeled
> ½ cup extra-virgin olive oil, or as needed

1. Build a charcoal fire in an outdoor grill and let burn until covered with white ash. Or preheat a gas grill on High.

2. Grill the bread, turning once, until lightly toasted, about 3 minutes. Rub each slice on one side with the garlic. Drizzle or brush the oil over the bread. Cut each slice crosswise into 3 or 4 pieces. (The bruschetta can be stored uncovered at room temperature for up to 2 hours.)

Herbed Breadsticks

makes 16 breadsticks

MAKE-AHEAD: The breadsticks can be prepared up to 1 day ahead.

Homemade breadsticks have a rustic look that is much more appealing than the staid store-bought variety. Herbs give these added flavor with sesame seeds on top for visual interest.

¼ cup warm (105° to 115°F) water
1 tablespoon honey
1¾ teaspoons active dry yeast
1 cup cool water
2 tablespoons extra-virgin olive oil, plus more for
    brushing
1 teaspoon dried basil
1 teaspoon dried oregano
½ teaspoon granulated garlic (coarse garlic powder)
1½ teaspoons kosher salt
4 cups unbleached all-purpose flour, or as needed
Yellow cornmeal for sprinkling
2 tablespoons sesame seeds

1.   Mix the warm water and honey in the bowl of a heavy-duty electric mixer. Sprinkle in the yeast and let stand until the mixture looks foamy, about 5 minutes.

2. Add the cool water, the oil, basil, oregano, granulated garlic, and salt. Attach the bowl to the mixer and fit with the paddle blade. Mix on low speed to dissolve the salt. Gradually add enough flour to make a soft dough that pulls away from the sides of the bowl. Change to the dough hook. Knead on medium speed until the dough is smooth, supple, and slightly sticky, about 5 minutes. Gather the dough into a ball, place it in a lightly oiled medium bowl, and turn to coat. Cover tightly with plastic wrap and let stand in a warm place until doubled in bulk, about 1¼ hours.

3. Position the racks in the top third and center of the oven and preheat the oven to 450°F. Sprinkle two large baking sheets with cornmeal.

4. Punch down the dough. Sprinkle a work surface with cornmeal, and pat and stretch out the dough into a 12 × 9-inch rectangle. Brush the top of the dough with water and sprinkle with the sesame seeds. Using a pizza wheel or sharp knife, cut the dough lengthwise into ½-inch-wide strips. Place the strips (they will stretch) about ½ inch apart on the baking sheets.

5. Immediately place in the oven and bake, switching the position of the racks from top to bottom after 6 minutes, until the breadsticks are golden brown, 8 to 10 minutes. Let cool completely. (The breadsticks can be wrapped in aluminum foil and stored at room temperature for up to 1 day.)

Index

beans (*continued*)

   soy, in miso-ginger, 106–7

   three-, salsa, 66–67

   white, and roasted garlic, 128–29

beef:

   beefed-up cheese, hot, 154–55

   and pinto bean chili, hot, 152–53

beet chips, 173

bell peppers:

   for dipping, 88

   roasted, 12

black bean and bacon, 74–75

black-eyed peas, in Texas caviar, 72–73

blue cheese dip, 32

   onion and, 17

bowls, 4, 6

brandade, smoked trout, 148–49

breadsticks, herbed, 184–85

broccoli:

   Cheddar and, 94–95

   classic cheese and, 95

   for dipping, 85

bruschetta, 132, 182–83

buttermilk-garlic dip, 36–37

C

Caesar dip, basil, 50

Cajun seasoning, 142–43

California dip, 16, 17

caper and Italian tuna spread, 150–51

caponata, 2, 33–35

carp roe, salted, 146–47

carrot:

   chips, 172

   for dipping, 85

   roasted, and peanut spread, 96–97

   -tahini, 124–25

cauliflower, for dipping, 85

caviar:

   Texas, 72–73

   Texas, with bacon, 73

   wild mushroom, 40–41

celery, for dipping, 85

Cheddar:

   bacon and, 156–57

   broccoli and, 94–95

cheese:

   classic broccoli and, 95

   hot beefed-up, 154–55

   see also specific cheeses

hummus (*continued*)
   herbed, 39
   red pepper, 39

I

Italian mama tomato and
   pepperoni dunk,
   160–61
Italian tuna and caper
   spread, 150–51

J

Jalapeño chiles, 9
   in red flame salsa, 64–65

L

Layered dips:
   classic seven-, 75
   ultimate Tex-Mex,
      74–75
leek-spinach dip, 21–22
Long Island clam dip,
   135–37
low-fat products, 5

M

Major Grey's chutney, 98,
   99

mascarpone-pesto dip,
   112–13
mayonnaise, 11
meat dips, 133–65
   antipasti salsa, 162–63
   bacon and Cheddar,
      156–57
   chicken liver and apple
      spread, 164–65
   ham and Swiss cheese
      spread, 145
   hot beef and pinto bean
      chili, 152–53
   hot beefed-up cheese,
      154–55
   Italian mama tomato and
      pepperoni dunk,
      160–61
   New Mexican pork and
      green chile,
      158–59
Mexican crema, 78–79
mint, zucchini, and garlic,
   130–31
miso-ginger dip, 106–7
Moroccan eggplant and
   tomato, 102–3
mushroom(s):
   for dipping, 86–87
   and Swiss, hot, 108–9
   wild, caviar, 40–41